William F. (William Fogg) Osgood

Introduction to Infinite Series

William F. (William Fogg) Osgood

Introduction to Infinite Series

ISBN/EAN: 9783743305144

Manufactured in Europe, USA, Canada, Australia, Japa

Cover: Foto ©ninafisch / pixelio.de

Manufactured and distributed by brebook publishing software (www.brebook.com)

William F. (William Fogg) Osgood

Introduction to Infinite Series

PREFACE.

IN an introductory course on the Differential and Integral Calculus the subject of Infinite Series forms an important topic. The presentation of this subject should have in view first to make the beginner acquainted with the nature and use of infinite series and secondly to introduce him to the theory of these series in such a way that he sees at each step precisely what the question at issue is and never enters on the proof of a theorem till he feels that the theorem actually requires proof. Aids to the attainment of these ends are: (*a*) a variety of illustrations, taken from the cases that actually arise in practice, of the application of series to computation both in pure and applied mathematics; (*b*) a full and careful exposition of the meaning and scope of the more difficult theorems; (*c*) the use of diagrams and graphical illustrations in the proofs.

The pamphlet that follows is designed to give a presentation of the kind here indicated. The references are to Byerly's *Differential Calculus*, *Integral Calculus*, and *Problems in Differential Calculus*; and to B. O. Peirce's *Short Table of Integrals*; all published by Ginn & Co., Boston.

WM. F. OSGOOD.

CAMBRIDGE, April 1897.

INTRODUCTION.

1. *Example.*—Consider the successive values of the variable

$$s_n = 1 + r + r^2 + \cdots\cdots + r^{n-1}$$

for $n = 1, 2, 3, \cdots\cdots$ Let r have the value $\frac{1}{2}$. Then

$$\begin{aligned} s_1 &= 1 &&= 1 \\ s_2 &= 1 + \tfrac{1}{2} &&= 1\tfrac{1}{2} \\ s_3 &= 1 + \tfrac{1}{2} + \tfrac{1}{4} &&= 1\tfrac{3}{4} \\ s_4 &= 1 + \tfrac{1}{2} + \tfrac{1}{4} + \tfrac{1}{8} &&= 1\tfrac{7}{8} \\ &\cdots\cdots \end{aligned}$$

If the values be represented by points on a line, it is easy to see the

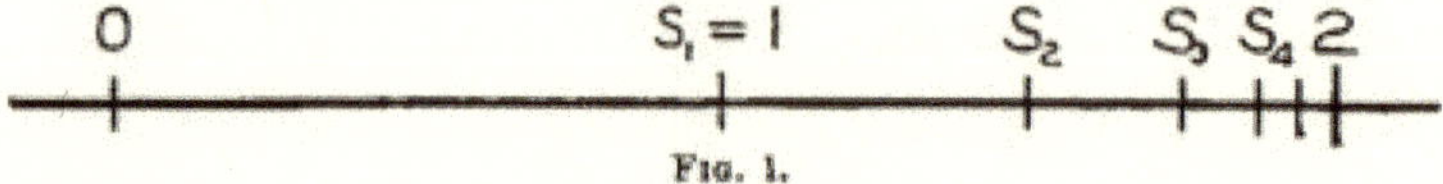

FIG. 1.

law by which any s_n can be obtained from its predecessor, s_{n-1}, namely: s_n lies half way between s_{n-1} and 2.

Hence it appears that when n increases without limit,

$$\text{Lim } s_n = 2.$$

The same result could have been obtained arithmetically from the formula for the sum s_n of the first n terms of the geometric series

$$a + ar + ar^2 + \cdots\cdots + ar^{n-1},$$

$$s_n = \frac{a(1 - r^n)}{1 - r}.$$

Here $a = 1$, $r = \frac{1}{2}$,

$$s_n = \frac{1 - \frac{1}{2^n}}{1 - \frac{1}{2}} = 2 - \frac{1}{2^{n-1}}.$$

When n increases without limit, $\frac{1}{2^{n-1}}$ approaches 0 as its limit, and hence as before $\text{Lim } s_n = 2$.

2. *Definition of an Infinite Series.* Let $u_0, u_1, u_2, \cdots\cdots$ be any set of values, positive or negative or both, and form the series

$$u_0 + u_1 + u_2 + \cdots\cdots \qquad (1)$$

Denote the sum of the first n terms by s_n:

$$s_n = u_0 + u_1 + \cdots\cdots + u_{n-1}.$$

Allow n to increase without limit. Then either a) s_n will approach a limit U:

$$\lim_{n=\infty} s_n = U;$$

or b) s_n approaches no limit. In either case we speak of (1) as an *Infinite Series*, because n is allowed to increase without limit. In case a) the infinite series is said to be *convergent* and to have the *value** U or *converge towards* the value U. In case b) the infinite series is said to be divergent.

The geometric series above considered is an example of a convergent series.

$$1 + 2 + 3 + \cdots\cdots,$$
$$1 - 1 + 1 - \cdots\cdots$$

are examples of divergent series. Only convergent series are of use in practice.

The notation

$$u_0 + u_1 + \cdots\cdots \textit{ ad inf.} \text{ (or } \textit{to infinity}\text{)}$$

is often used for the limit U, or simply

$$U = u_0 + u_1 + \cdots\cdots$$

* U is often called the *sum* of the series. But the student must not forget that U is *not* a sum, but is the *limit* of a sum. Similarly the expression "the sum of an infinite number of terms" means the *limit* of the sum of n of these terms, as n increases without limit.

I. CONVERGENCE.

a) SERIES, ALL OF WHOSE TERMS ARE POSITIVE.

3. *Example.* Let it be required to test the convergence of the series

$$1 + 1 + \frac{1}{1\cdot 2} + \frac{1}{1\cdot 2\cdot 3} + \cdots\cdots + \frac{1}{n!} + \cdots\cdots \quad (2)$$

where $n!$ means $1\cdot 2\cdot 3\cdot\cdots\cdots\cdot n$ and is read "*factorial n*". Discarding for the moment the first term, compare the sum of the next n terms

$$\sigma_n = 1 + \frac{1}{1\cdot 2} + \frac{1}{1\cdot 2\cdot 3} + \cdots\cdots + \frac{1}{1\cdot 2\cdot 3\cdot\cdots\cdots\cdot n}$$

with the corresponding sum

$$S_n = 1 + \frac{1}{2} + \frac{1}{2\cdot 2} + \cdots\cdots + \frac{1}{\underbrace{2\cdot 2\cdot 2\cdot\cdots\cdots\cdot 2}_{n-1 \text{ factors}}}$$

$$= 2 - \frac{1}{2^{n-1}} < 2 \quad (\text{Cf. § 1}).$$

Each term of σ_n after the first two is less than the corresponding term in S_n, and hence the sum

$$\sigma_n < S_n < 2,$$

or, inserting the discarded term and denoting the sum of the first n terms of the given series by s_n,

$$s_{n+1} = 1 + 1 + \frac{1}{1\cdot 2} + \frac{1}{1\cdot 2\cdot 3} + \cdots\cdots + \frac{1}{1\cdot 2\cdot 3\cdots\cdots n} < 3,$$

no matter how large n be taken. That is to say, s_n is a variable that always increases as n increases, but that never attains so large a value as 3. To make these relations clear to the eye, plot the successive values of s_n as points on a line.

$$s_1 = 1 \qquad\qquad = 1.$$

$$s_2 = 1 + 1 \qquad\qquad = 2.$$

$$s_3 = 1 + 1 + \frac{1}{2!} \qquad\qquad = 2.5$$

$$s_4 = 1 + 1 + \frac{1}{2!} + \frac{1}{3!} \qquad\qquad = 2.667$$

$$s_5 = 1 + 1 + \frac{1}{2!} + \frac{1}{3!} + \frac{1}{4!} \qquad\qquad = 2.708$$

$$s_6 = 1 + 1 + \frac{1}{2!} + \frac{1}{3!} + \frac{1}{4!} + \frac{1}{5!} \qquad\qquad = 2.717$$

$$s_7 = 1 + 1 + \frac{1}{2!} + \frac{1}{3!} + \frac{1}{4!} + \frac{1}{5!} + \frac{1}{6!} \qquad\qquad = 2.718$$

$$s_8 = 1 + 1 + \frac{1}{2!} + \frac{1}{3!} + \frac{1}{4!} + \frac{1}{5!} + \frac{1}{6!} + \frac{1}{7!} = 2.718$$

0 $S_1 = 1$ $S_2 = 2$ S_3 e 3

FIG. 2.

When n increases by 1, the point representing s_{n+1} always moves to the right, but never advances so far as the point 3. *Hence there must be some point e, either coinciding with 3 or lying to the left of 3 (i.e. $e \leqq 3$), which s_n approaches as its limit, but never reaches.* To judge from the values computed for $s_1, s_2, \cdots s_8$, the value of e to three places of decimals is 2.718, a fact that will be established later.

4. Fundamental Principle. The reasoning by which we have here inferred the *existence* of a limit e, although we do not as yet know how to *compute the numerical value* of that limit, is of prime importance for the work that follows. Let us state it clearly in general form.

If s_n is a variable that 1) *always increases when n increases:*

$$s_{n'} > s_n, \qquad\qquad n' > n;$$

but that 2) *always remains less than some definite fixed number, A:*

$$s_n < A$$

for all values of n, then s_n approaches a limit, U:

$$\lim_{n=\infty} s_n = U.$$

This limit, U, is not greater than A:

$$U \leqq A.$$

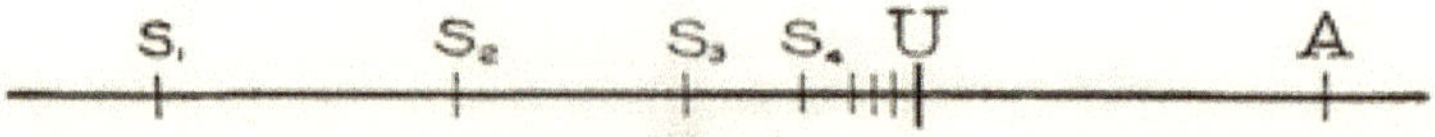

Fig. 3.

The value A may be the limit itself or any value greater than the limit.

Exercise. State the Principle for a variable that is always *decreasing*, but is always *greater* than a certain fixed quantity, and draw the corresponding figure.

5. *First Test for Convergence. Direct Comparison.* On the principle of the preceding paragraph is based the following test for the convergence of an infinite series.

Let
$$u_0 + u_1 + u_2 + \cdots\cdots \qquad (\alpha)$$
be a series of positive terms, the convergence of which it is desired to test. If a series of positive terms already known to be convergent
$$a_0 + a_1 + a_2 + \cdots\cdots \qquad (\beta)$$
can be found whose terms are never less than the corresponding terms in the series to be tested (α), *then* (α) *is a convergent series, and its value does not exceed that of the series* (β).

For let
$$s_n = u_0 + u_1 + \cdots\cdots + u_{n-1},$$
$$S_n = a_0 + a_1 + \cdots\cdots + a_{n-1},$$
$$\lim_{n=\infty} S_n = A.$$

Then since $\quad S_n < A \quad$ and $\quad s_n \leqq S_n,$

it follows that $\quad s_n < A$

and hence by §4 s_n approaches a limit and this limit is not greater than A.

Remark. It is frequently convenient in studying the convergence of a series to discard a few terms at the beginning (m, say, when m is a *fixed* number) and to consider the new series thus arising. That the convergence of this series is necessary and sufficient for the convergence of the original series is evident, since

$$s_n = (u_0 + \cdots\cdots + u_{m-1}) + (u_m + \cdots\cdots + u_{n-1})$$
$$= \qquad \bar{u} \qquad + \qquad \bar{s}_{n-m}.$$

$\bar{u}$ is constant and hence s_n will converge toward a limit if $\bar{s}_{n-m}$ does, and conversely.

Examples. Prove the following series convergent.

$$1 + \frac{1}{2^2} + \frac{1}{3^3} + \frac{1}{4^4} + \cdots\cdots$$

$$r + r^4 + r^9 + r^{16} + \cdots\cdots, \qquad 0 < r < 1$$

$$\frac{1}{3\,!} + \frac{1}{5\,!} + \frac{1}{7\,!} + \cdots\cdots$$

$$\frac{1}{1\cdot 2} + \frac{1}{2\cdot 3} + \frac{1}{3\cdot 4} + \cdots\cdots$$

Solution. Write s_n in the form

$$s_n = \left(1 - \frac{1}{2}\right) + \left(\frac{1}{2} - \frac{1}{3}\right) + \cdots\cdots + \left(\frac{1}{n} - \frac{1}{n+1}\right)$$
$$= 1 - \frac{1}{n+1};$$

then

$$\lim_{n=\infty} s_n = 1.$$

$$\frac{1}{1\cdot 2} + \frac{1}{3\cdot 4} + \frac{1}{5\cdot 6} + \cdots\cdots$$

$$1 + \frac{1}{2^2} + \frac{1}{3^2} + \frac{1}{4^2} + \cdots\cdots$$

$$1 + \frac{1}{2^p} + \frac{1}{3^p} + \cdots\cdots, \qquad p > 2.$$

6. *A New Test-Series.* It has just been seen that the series

$$1 + \frac{1}{2^p} + \frac{1}{3^p} + \frac{1}{4^p} + \cdots\cdots \tag{3}$$

converges when the constant quantity $p \geqq 2$. We will now prove that it also converges whenever $p > 1$. The truth of the following inequalities is at once evident:

$$\frac{1}{2^p} + \frac{1}{3^p} < \frac{2}{2^p} = \frac{1}{2^{p-1}}$$

$$\frac{1}{4^p} + \frac{1}{5^p} + \frac{1}{6^p} + \frac{1}{7^p} < \frac{4}{4^p} = \frac{1}{4^{p-1}}$$

$$\frac{1}{8^p} + \frac{1}{9^p} + \cdots\cdots + \frac{1}{15^p} < \frac{8}{8^p} = \frac{1}{8^{p-1}}$$

Hence, adding m of these inequalities together, we get

$$\frac{1}{2^p} + \frac{1}{3^p} + \cdots\cdots + \frac{1}{(2^{m+1} - 1)^p} < \frac{1}{2^{p-1}} + \frac{1}{4^{p-1}} + \frac{1}{8^{p-1}} + \cdots\cdots + \frac{1}{(2^m)^{p-1}}.$$

Denote $1/2^{p-1}$ by r; then, since $p - 1 > 0$, $r < 1$ and the series

$$\frac{1}{2^{p-1}} + \frac{1}{4^{p-1}} + \frac{1}{8^{p-1}} + \cdots\cdots = r + r^2 + r^3 + \cdots\cdots$$

converges toward the limit $\frac{r}{1 - r}$. Consequently no matter how many terms of the series

$$\frac{1}{2^p} + \frac{1}{3^p} + \frac{1}{4^p} + \cdots\cdots$$

be taken, their sum will always be less than $\frac{r}{1 - r}$, and this series is therefore convergent, by the principle of § 4.

Series (3) is useful as a test-series, for many series that could not be shown to be convergent by the aid of the geometric series, can be so shown by reference to it. For example,

$$1 + \frac{1}{2\sqrt{2}} + \frac{1}{3\sqrt{3}} + \frac{1}{4\sqrt{4}} + \cdots\cdots.$$

7. *Divergent Series.* The series (3) has been proved convergent for *every* value of $p > 1$. Thus the series

$$1 + \frac{1}{2\sqrt[100]{2}} + \frac{1}{3\sqrt[100]{3}} + \frac{1}{4\sqrt[100]{4}} + \cdots\cdots$$

is a convergent series, for $p = 1.01$. Now consider what the numerical values of these roots in the denominators are:

$$\sqrt[100]{2} = 1.007, \quad \sqrt[100]{3} = 1.011, \quad \sqrt[100]{4} = 1.014.$$

In fact $\sqrt[100]{100} = 1.047$ and $\sqrt[100]{1000} = 1.071$; that is, when a thousand terms of the series have been taken, the denominator of the last term is multiplied by a number so slightly different from 1 that the first significant figure of the decimal part appears only in the second place. And when one considers that these same relations will be still more strongly marked when p is set equal to 1.001 or 1.0001, one may well ask whether the series obtained by putting $p = 1$,

$$1 + \frac{1}{2} + \frac{1}{3} + \frac{1}{4} + \cdots\cdots \qquad (4)$$

is not also convergent.

This is however not the case. For

$$\frac{1}{n+1} + \frac{1}{n+2} + \cdots\cdots + \frac{1}{n+n} > n\frac{1}{2n} = \frac{1}{2},$$

since each of the n terms, save the last, is greater than $1/2n$. Hence we can strike in in the series anywhere, add a definite number of terms together and thus get a sum greater than $\frac{1}{2}$, and we can do this as often as we please. For example,

$$n = 2, \qquad \frac{1}{3} + \frac{1}{4} > \frac{1}{2}$$

$$n = 4, \qquad \frac{1}{5} + \frac{1}{6} + \frac{1}{7} + \frac{1}{8} > \frac{1}{2}$$

$$n = 8, \qquad \frac{1}{9} + \frac{1}{10} + \cdots\cdots + \frac{1}{16} > \frac{1}{2}$$

. . . .

Hence the sum of the first n terms increases without limit as n increases without limit,

or

$$\lim_{n=\infty} s_n = \infty$$

The series (4) is called the harmonic series.

How is the apparently sudden change from convergence for $p > 1$ in series (3) to divergence when $p = 1$ to be accounted for? The explanation is simple. When p is only slightly greater than 1, series (3) indeed converges still, but it converges towards a *large* value, and this value, which is of course a function of p, increases without limit when p, decreasing, approaches 1. When $p = 1$, no limit exists, and the series is divergent.

8. *Test for Divergence. Exercise.* Establish the test for divergence of a series corresponding to the test of §5 for convergence, namely: *Let*

$$u_0 + u_1 + \cdots\cdots \qquad (\alpha)$$

be a series of positive terms that is to be tested for divergence. If a series of positive terms already known to be divergent

$$a_0 + a_1 + \cdots\cdots \qquad (\beta)$$

can be found whose terms are never greater than the corresponding terms in the series to be tested (α), *then* (α) *is a divergent series.*

Examples.

$$1 + \frac{1}{\sqrt{2}} + \frac{1}{\sqrt{3}} + \frac{1}{\sqrt{4}} + \cdots\cdots$$

$$1+\frac{1}{2^p}+\frac{1}{3^p}+\frac{1}{4^p}+\cdots\cdots \qquad p<1$$

$$1+\frac{1}{3}+\frac{1}{5}+\frac{1}{7}+\cdots\cdots$$

This last series can be proved divergent by reference to the series

$$\frac{1}{2}+\frac{1}{4}+\frac{1}{6}+\cdots\cdots$$

Let
$$s_n=\frac{1}{2}+\frac{1}{4}+\frac{1}{6}+\cdots\cdots+\frac{1}{2n}$$
$$=\frac{1}{2}\left(1+\frac{1}{2}+\frac{1}{3}+\cdots\cdots+\frac{1}{n}\right).$$

The series in parenthesis is the harmonic series, and its sum increases without limit as n increases; hence s_n increases without limit and the series is divergent.

9. *Second Test for Convergence. The Test-Ratio.* Let the series to be tested be

$$u_0+u_1+\cdots\cdots+u_n+\cdots\cdots$$

and form the test-ratio

$$\frac{u_{n+1}}{u_n}.$$

When n increases without limit, this ratio will in general approach a definite fixed limit (or increase without limit). Call the limit τ. *Then if* $\tau<1$ *the series is convergent, if* $\tau>1$, *it is divergent, if* $\tau=1$ *there is no test:*

$$\lim_{n=\infty}\frac{u_{n+1}}{u_n}=\tau<1, \text{ Convergent;}$$
$$\text{“} \qquad \tau>1, \text{ Divergent;}$$
$$\text{“} \qquad \tau=1, \text{ No Test.}$$

First, let $\tau<1$. Then as n increases, the points corresponding to the values of u_{n+1}/u_n will cluster about the point τ, and hence if

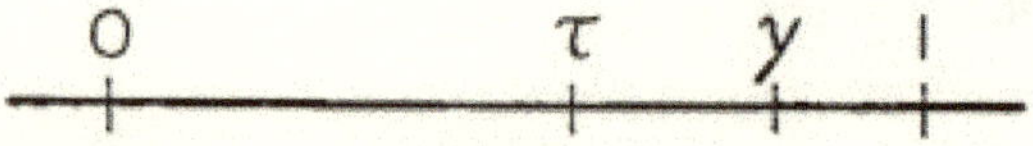

O τ γ 1

Fig. 4.

a fixed point γ be chosen at pleasure between τ and 1, the points u_{n+1}/u_n will, for sufficiently large values of n, i.e. for all values of n equal to or greater than a certain fixed number m, lie to the left of γ, and we shall have

$$\frac{u_{n+1}}{u_n} < \gamma, \qquad n \geqq m;$$

or, $n = m$, $\quad \frac{u_{m+1}}{u_m} < \gamma, \quad u_{m+1} < u_m \gamma,$

$n = m + 1, \quad \frac{u_{m+2}}{u_{m+1}} < \gamma, \quad u_{m+2} < u_{m+1}\gamma < u_m \gamma^2,$

$n = m + 2, \quad \frac{u_{m+3}}{u_{m+2}} < \gamma, \quad u_{m+3} < u_{m+2}\gamma < u_m \gamma^3,$

. . . .

Adding p of these inequalities, we get

$$u_{m+1} + u_{m+2} + u_{m+3} + \cdots\cdots + u_{m+p}$$
$$< u_m(\gamma + \gamma^2 + \gamma^3 + \cdots\cdots + \gamma^p) < u_m \frac{\gamma}{1-\gamma}.$$

The sum of the terms u, beginning with u_{m+1} never, therefore, rises as high as the value $u_m \frac{\gamma}{1-\gamma}$. Hence the u-series converges.

The case that $\tau > 1$ (or $\tau = \infty$) is treated in a similar manner, and may be left as an exercise for the student.

If $\tau = 1$ there is no test. For consider series (3). The test-ratio is

$$\frac{u_{n+1}}{u_n} = \frac{n^p}{(n+1)^p} = \left(1 + \frac{1}{n}\right)^{-p}$$

and hence $\tau = 1$, no matter what value p may have. But when $p > 1$, (3) converges; and when $p < 1$, (3) diverges. Thus it appears that τ can equal 1 both for convergent and for divergent series.

Remark. The student will observe that the theorem does *not* say that the series will converge if u_{n+1}/u_n becomes and remains less than 1 when n increases, but that it demands that the *limit* of u_{n+1}/u_n shall be less than 1. Thus in the case of the harmonic series this ratio $n/(n+1)$ is less than 1 for all values of n, and yet the series diverges. But the *limit* is not less than 1.

Examples. Are the following series convergent or divergent?

$$\frac{1}{3} + \frac{1}{3}\cdot\frac{2}{5} + \frac{1}{3}\cdot\frac{2}{5}\cdot\frac{3}{7} + \cdots\cdots$$

$$\frac{1}{2} + \frac{2}{2^2} + \frac{3}{2^3} + \frac{4}{2^4} + \cdots\cdots$$

$$\frac{2}{2^{100}} + \frac{2^2}{3^{100}} + \frac{2^3}{4^{100}} + \cdots\cdots$$

$$\frac{2!}{100} + \frac{3!}{100^2} + \frac{4!}{100^3} + \cdots\cdots$$

10. *A Further Test-Ratio Test.* The following test for convergence and divergence is sometimes useful; the proof of the rule is omitted. If

$$n\left(1-\frac{u_{n+1}}{u_n}\right)$$

approaches a limit, let this limit be denoted by σ. *Then the series*

$$u_0+u_1+\cdots\cdots$$

converges, if $\sigma > 1$ (*or if* $\sigma = \infty$);

diverges, if $\sigma < 1$ (*or if* $\sigma = -\infty$);

if $\sigma = 1$, *there is no test.*

Example.

$$\frac{1}{1\cdot 2}+\frac{1}{3\cdot 4}+\cdots\cdots$$

$$n\left(1-\frac{u_{n+1}}{u_n}\right)=n\left(1-\frac{(n-1)\,n}{n\,(n+1)}\right)=\frac{2}{1+\frac{1}{n}}$$

and $\sigma = 2$; the series converges.

Test the following series:

$$\frac{1}{2}+\frac{1\cdot 3}{2\cdot 4}+\frac{1\cdot 3\cdot 5}{2\cdot 4\cdot 6}+\cdots\cdots$$

$$\left(\frac{1}{2}\right)^3+\left(\frac{1\cdot 3}{2\cdot 4}\right)^3+\left(\frac{1\cdot 3\cdot 5}{2\cdot 4\cdot 6}\right)^3+\cdots\cdots$$

$$\frac{1}{2^2-a}+\frac{1}{3^2-a}+\frac{1}{4^2-a}+\cdots\cdots$$

Apply any of the foregoing tests to determine the convergence or the divergence of the series on pp. 45, 46 of Byerly's *Problems in Differential Calculus.*

b) SERIES WITH BOTH POSITIVE AND NEGATIVE TERMS.

11. *Alternating Series. Theorem. Let the terms of the given series* 1) *be alternately positive and negative:*

$$u_0-u_1+u_2-u_3+\cdots\cdots; \qquad (5)$$

2) *let each u be less than (or equal to) its predecessor:*

$$u_{n+1} \leqq u_n;$$

3) *let*

$$\lim_{n=\infty} u_n = 0.$$

Then the series is convergent.

The following series may serve as an example.

$$1-\frac{1}{2}+\frac{1}{3}-\frac{1}{4}+\cdots\cdots \tag{6}$$

Proof. Let

$$s_n = u_0 - u_1 + u_2 \cdots\cdots + (-1)^{n-1}u_{n-1}$$

and plot the points $s_1, s_2, s_3, \cdots\cdots$ Then we shall show that the points $s_1, s_3, s_5, \cdots\cdots s_{2m+1}, \cdots\cdots$ always move to the left,

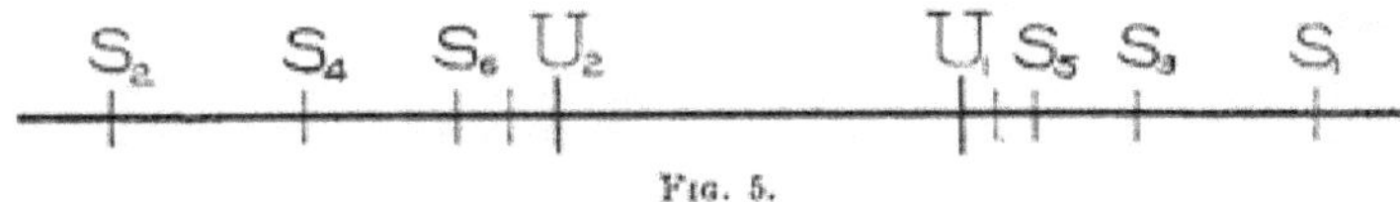

Fig. 5.

but never advance so far to the left as s_2, for example. Hence by the principle of § 4 they approach a limit, U_1:

$$\lim_{m=\infty} s_{2m+1} = U_1.$$

Similarly, the points $s_2, s_4, s_6, \cdots\cdots s_{2m}, \cdots\cdots$ always move to the right, but never advance so far to the right as s_1, for example; hence by the same principle they also approach a limit, U_2:

$$\lim_{m=\infty} s_{2m} = U_2.$$

Finally, since

$$s_{2m+1} = s_{2m} + u_{2m},$$

$$\lim_{m=\infty} s_{2m+1} = \lim_{m=\infty} s_{2m} + \lim_{m=\infty} u_{2m};$$

but $\lim u_{2m} = 0$; — here the third hypothesis of the theorem comes into play for the first time; — hence

$$U_1 = U_2,$$

or simply U. Thus s_n approaches a limit, U, continually springing over its limit.

Fig. 6.

Such is the reasoning of the proof. It remains to supply the analytical establishment of the facts on which this reasoning depends.

First, $\qquad s_{2m+1} \leqq s_{2m-1} \qquad$ and $\qquad s_{2m} \geqq s_{2m-2}.$

For $s_{2m+1} = u_0 - (u_1 - u_2) - \cdots\cdots - (u_{2m-3} - u_{2m-2}) - (u_{2m-1} - u_{2m})$

$$= s_{2m-1} - (u_{2m-1} - u_{2m});$$

$$s_{2m} = (u_0 - u_1) + \cdots\cdots + (u_{2m-4} - u_{2m-3}) + (u_{2m-2} - u_{2m-1})$$

$$= s_{2m-2} + (u_{2m-2} - u_{2m-1});$$

and the parentheses are all positive (or null).

Next $$s_{2m+1} > s_2 \qquad \text{and} \qquad s_{2m} < s_1.$$
For
$$s_{2m+1} = s_{2m} + u_{2m} \geqq s_2 + u_{2m} > s_2,$$
$$s_{2m} = s_{2m-1} - u_{2m} \leqq s_1 - u_{2m} < s_1.$$
The proof is now complete.

Examples.

$$1 - \frac{1}{3^2} + \frac{1}{5^2} - \frac{1}{7^2} + \cdots\cdots$$

$$\frac{1}{\log 2} - \frac{1}{\log 3} + \frac{1}{\log 4} - \cdots\cdots$$

12. *The Limit of Error in the Alternating Series.* Suppose it be required to find the value of series (5) correct to k, say, to 3 places of decimals.

For this purpose it is not enough to know merely that the series converges, and hence that *enough* terms *can* be taken so that their sum s_n will differ from the limit U by less than .001, for n might be so great, say greater than 10,000, that it would be out of the question to compute s_n. And in any case one must know when it is safe to stop adding terms.

The rule here is extremely simple. *The sum of the first n terms of series (5), s_n, differs from the value of the series, U, by less than the numerical value of the $(n+1)$st term.* In other words, we may stop adding terms as soon as we come to a term which is numerically smaller than the proposed limit of error.

For, consider Fig. (6). The transition from s_n to s_{n+1} consists in the addition to s_n of a quantity numerically greater than the distance from s_n to U. This quantity is precisely the $(n+1)$st term of the series. Hence the rule.

For example, let it be required to compute the value of the series

$$\frac{1}{3} - \frac{1}{2}\cdot\frac{1}{3^2} + \frac{1}{3}\cdot\frac{1}{3^3} - \frac{1}{4}\cdot\frac{1}{3^4} + \cdots\cdots \qquad (7)$$

correct to three places of decimals.

$$\begin{array}{rlrl}
(\tfrac{1}{3}) &= .3333 & \tfrac{1}{2}(\tfrac{1}{3})^2 &= .0556 \\
\tfrac{1}{3}(\tfrac{1}{3})^3 &= .0123 & \tfrac{1}{4}(\tfrac{1}{3})^4 &= .0031 \\
\tfrac{1}{5}(\tfrac{1}{3})^5 &= .0008 & \tfrac{1}{6}(\tfrac{1}{3})^6 &= .0002 \\
\tfrac{1}{7}(\tfrac{1}{3})^7 &= .0000 & & \overline{.0589} \\
& \overline{.3464} & &
\end{array}$$

$$.3464 - .0589 = .2875$$

or, to 3 places, the value of series (7) is .288.*

* The 4th place is retained throughout the work to insure accuracy in the third place in the final result.

Examples. 1. Show that the value of the series

$$\frac{1}{2} - \frac{1}{2}\,\frac{1}{2^2} + \frac{1}{3}\,\frac{1}{2^3} - \frac{1}{4}\,\frac{1}{2^4} + \frac{1}{5}\,\frac{1}{2^5} \cdots\cdots$$

to three places of decimals is .405.

2. How many terms of the series

$$1 - \frac{1}{2} + \frac{1}{3} - \frac{1}{4} + \cdots\cdots$$

would have to be taken that the sum might represent the value of the series correct to 3 places of decimals?

13. *A General Theorem. Let*

$$u_0 + u_1 + \cdots\cdots$$

be any convergent series of positive and negative terms. Then

$$\lim_{n=\infty} u_n = 0 .$$

More generally,

$$\lim_{n=\infty} [u_n + u_{n+1} + \cdots\cdots + u_{n+p-1}] = 0 ,$$

where p is any integer, either constant or varying with n.

The proof of this theorem flows directly out of the conception of a limit. Let

$$s_n = u_0 + u_1 + \cdots\cdots + u_{n-1}$$

and plot the points $s_1, s_2, s_3, \cdots\cdots$ Then what we mean when we say "*s_n approaches a limit U*" is that there is a point U about which the s_n's cluster, as n increases. This does not necessarily require that (as in the series hitherto considered) s_n should always come steadily nearer to U, as n increases. Thus s_3 may lie further away from U than s_2 does. But it does mean that ultimately the s_n's will

S_3 $U-\delta$ S_4 U S_2 $U+\delta$ S_1

FIG. 7.

cease to deviate from U by more than any arbitrarily assigned quantity, δ, however small. In other words, let δ be taken at pleasure ($= 1/1,000,000$, say) and lay off an interval extending to a distance δ from U in each direction, $(U - \delta, U + \delta)$; then for the larger values of n, more precisely, for all values of n greater than a certain fixed number m, s_n will lie within this interval. This can be stated algebraically in the following form:

$$U - \delta < s_n < U + \delta, \qquad \text{when } n > m.$$

Having thus stated what is meant by s_n's approaching a limit U, we now turn to the proof of the theorem. The sum

$$u_n + u_{n+1} + \cdots\cdots + u_{n+p-1} = s_{n+p} - s_n.$$

If $n > m$, both s_n and s_{n+p} will lie in the interval $(U - \delta, U + \delta)$. The distance between these points is therefore less than 2δ. Hence

$$-2\delta < u_n + u_{n+1} + \cdots\cdots + u_{n+p-1} < 2\delta,$$

no matter what value p may have. But if a quantity depends on n and can be made to remain numerically as small as is desired by increasing n, then it approaches 0 as its limit, when $n = \infty$. Thus the proposition is established.

It is to be noticed that while the condition $\text{Lim}\, u_n = 0$ is *necessary*, if the series is to converge, it is in no wise *sufficient* for the convergence. Thus in the harmonic series (4) the general term approaches 0 as its limit, but still the series diverges. The harmonic series however does not satisfy the more general condition of the theorem; for if we put $p = n$,

$$u_n + u_{n+1} + \cdots\cdots + u_{n+p-1} = \frac{1}{n+1} + \frac{1}{n+2} + \cdots\cdots + \frac{1}{n+n} > \frac{1}{2}$$

and does not converge toward 0 as its limit. This fact affords a new proof of the divergence of the harmonic series.

It may be remarked that the more general condition

$$\lim_{n=\infty} [u_n + u_{n+1} + \cdots\cdots + u_{n+p-1}] = 0,$$

where p may vary with n *in any wise we choose*, is a sufficient condition for the convergence of the series. See Appendix.

14. *Convergence. The General Case.* Let

$$u_0 + u_1 + \cdots\cdots \qquad (a)$$

be any series and let

$$v_0 + v_1 + \cdots\cdots$$

denote the series of positive terms,

$$-w_0 - w_1 - \cdots\cdots$$

the series of negative terms, taken respectively in the order in which they occur in (a). For example, if the u-series is

$$1 - \frac{1}{2} + \frac{1}{2^2} - \frac{1}{2^3} + \cdots\cdots$$

then the v-series is

$$1 + \frac{1}{2^2} + \frac{1}{2^4} + \cdots\cdots$$

and the $-w$-series is

$$-\frac{1}{2} - \frac{1}{2^3} - \frac{1}{2^5} - \cdots\cdots.$$

Let

$$s_n = u_0 + u_1 + \cdots\cdots + u_{n-1},$$
$$\sigma_m = v_0 + v_1 + \cdots\cdots + v_{m-1},$$
$$\tau_p = w_0 + w_1 + \cdots\cdots + w_{p-1},$$

Then, whatever value n may have, s_n can be written in the form

$$s_n = \sigma_m - \tau_p.$$

Here m denotes the number of positive terms in s_n, σ_m their sum, etc. When n increases without limit, both m and p increase without limit, and two cases can arise.

Case I. Both σ_m and τ_p approach limits:

$$\lim_{m=\infty} \sigma_m = V, \qquad \lim_{p=\infty} \tau_p = W;$$

so that both the v-series and the w-series are convergent. Hence the u-series will also converge,

$$\lim_{n=\infty} s_n = U,$$

and

$$U = V - W.$$

The above example comes under this case. Case I will be of principal interest to us.

Case II. At least one of the variables σ_m, τ_p, approaches no limit. For example, suppose the u-series were

$$1 - \frac{1}{3^1} + \frac{1}{3} - \frac{1}{3^2} + \frac{1}{5} - \frac{1}{3^3} + \frac{1}{7} - \cdots\cdots$$

or

$$1 - \frac{1}{2} + \frac{1}{3} - \frac{1}{4} + \frac{1}{5} - \frac{1}{6} + \frac{1}{7} - \cdots\cdots$$

As these examples show, the u-series may then be convergent and it may be divergent.

Exercise. Show that if the u-series converges and one of the v-, w-series diverges, the other must also diverge.

Let us now form the series of *absolute values** of the terms of the

* By the *absolute value* of a real number is meant the numerical value of that number. Thus the absolute value of -3 is 3; of $2\frac{1}{2}$ is $2\frac{1}{2}$. Graphically it means the *distance* of the point representing that number from the point 0.

u-series and write this series as

$$u'_0 + u'_1 + \cdot \cdot \cdot \cdot \cdot$$

u'_n will be a certain v, if u_n is positive; a certain w, if u_n is negative. If we set

$$s'_n = u'_0 + u'_1 + \cdot \cdot \cdot \cdot \cdot + u'_{n-1}$$

it is clear that

$$s'_n = \sigma_m + \tau_p.$$

From this relation we deduce at once that in Case I the u'-series *is a convergent series.*

Conversely, *if the u'-series converges, then both the v-series and the w-series converge, and we have Case I.*

For both the v-series and the w-series are series of positive terms, and no matter how many terms be added in either series, the sum cannot exceed the limit U' toward which s'_n converges. Hence by the principle of § 4 each of these series converges.

Definition. Series whose absolute value series are convergent (i. e. u-series whose u'-series converge) are said to be *absolutely* or *unconditionally* convergent; other convergent series are said to be *not absolutely* convergent or *conditionally* convergent. The reason for the terminology *unconditionally* and *conditionally* convergent will appear in § 34.

15. *Test for Convergence.* Since the u-series surely converges if the u'-series converges — it is then absolutely convergent — and since the u'-series is a series made up exclusively of positive terms, the tests for convergence obtained in I. *a*) can be applied to the u'-series and from its convergence the convergence of the u-series can thus be inferred. The series that occur most frequently in elementary analysis either come under this head and can be proved convergent in the manner just indicated, or they belong to the class of alternating series considered in § 11.

The test of § 9 can be thrown into simpler form whenever the test-ratio u_{n+1}/u_n approaches a limit, t; the rule being that *when t is numerically less than 1, the series converges absolutely; when t is numerically greater than 1, the series diverges; when t is numerically equal to 1, there is no test:*

$$\lim_{n=\infty} \frac{u_{n+1}}{u_n} = t, \quad \begin{cases} -1 < t < 1, & \textit{Convergence;} \\ t > 1 \text{ or } t < -1, & \textit{Divergence;} \\ t = 1 \text{ or } t = -1, & \textit{No Test.} \end{cases}$$

For, the test-ratio u_{n+1}/u_n is numerically equal to the test-ratio of the series of absolute values, u'_{n+1}/u'_n. Now if a variable $f(n)$ approaches a limit, H, when $n = \infty$, its numerical value, being the *distance* of the point representing $f(n)$ from the point 0, approaches a limit too, namely the numerical value of H (distance of H from 0). Hence

$$\lim_{n=\infty} \frac{u'_{n+1}}{u'_n} = \tau,$$

where τ equals the numerical value of t. If then $-1 < t < 1$, it follows that $\tau < 1$ and the u'-series converges. The u-series is then absolutely convergent.

The second part of the rule will be proven in the next paragraph.

Example. Consider the series

$$x - \frac{x^2}{2} + \frac{x^3}{3} - \frac{x^4}{4} + \cdots\cdots$$

$$\frac{u_{n+1}}{u_n} = -\frac{x^{n+1}}{n+1} \cdot \frac{n}{x^n} = -\frac{1}{1+\frac{1}{n}} x$$

$$\operatorname*{Lim}_{n=\infty} \frac{u_{n+1}}{u_n} = t = -x.$$

Hence the series will converge when x is numerically less than 1, i. e. when

$$-1 < x < 1.$$

When $x = 1$ or -1, this test fails to give any information concerning the convergence of the series. But it is then seen directly that in the first case the series is convergent, in the second case, divergent.

16. *Divergence.* To establish the divergence of a series

$$u_0 + u_1 + \cdots\cdots$$

with positive and negative terms, it is not enough to establish the divergence of the u'-series, as the example of the series

$$1 - \frac{1}{2} + \frac{1}{3} - \frac{1}{4} + \cdots\cdots$$

shows. It will however suffice to show that the terms do not approach 0 as their limit, and this can frequently be done most conveniently by showing that the terms of the u'-series do not approach 0.

Thus if $\quad t > 1 \quad$ or $\quad t < -1, \quad$ then $\quad \tau > 1$

and $$\frac{u'_{n+1}}{u'_n} > 1, \qquad \text{when} \qquad n \geqq m.$$

Hence
$$u'_{m+1} > u'_m,$$
$$u'_{m+2} > u'_{m+1} > u'_m,$$
$$u'_{m+3} > u'_{m+2} > u'_m,$$
$$\cdot \quad \cdot \quad \cdot \quad \cdot \quad \cdot$$

or
$$u_n > u'_m, \qquad n > m;$$

that is, all the u'_n's from $n = m$ on are greater than a certain positive quantity $\rho = u'_m$ and hence u'_n and u_n cannot approach 0 as their limit, when $n = \infty$.

Example. In the series of § 15, $t = -x$; hence this series diverges for all values of x numerically greater than 1. These results may be represented graphically as follows:—

Divergent -1 0 1 *Divergent*
Convergent

Exercise. For what values of x are the following series convergent, for what values divergent? Indicate these values by a diagram similar to the one above.

$$x + \frac{x^2}{\sqrt{2}} + \frac{x^3}{\sqrt{3}} + \cdot \cdot \cdot \cdot \cdot$$

Ans. $-1 \leqq x < 1$, Conv.; $x \geqq 1$, $x < -1$, Div.

$$x - \frac{x^3}{3} + \frac{x^5}{5} - \frac{x^7}{7} + \cdot \cdot \cdot \cdot \cdot$$

$$1 + x + \frac{x^2}{2!} + \frac{x^3}{3!} + \cdot \cdot \cdot \cdot \cdot$$

$$x + 3^{117}x^3 + 5^{117}x^5 + 7^{117}x^7 + \cdot \cdot \cdot \cdot \cdot$$

$$10x + 10^2x^2 + 10^3x^3 + \cdot \cdot \cdot \cdot \cdot$$

$$1 + x + 2!\,x^2 + 3!\,x^3 + \cdot \cdot \cdot \cdot \cdot$$

17. THEOREM. *Let*

$$a_0 + a_1 + a_2 + \cdot \cdot \cdot \cdot \cdot$$

be any absolutely convergent series; $\rho_0, \rho_1, \rho_2, \cdot \cdot \cdot \cdot \cdot$ any set of quantities not increasing numerically indefinitely. Then the series

$$a_0\rho_0 + a_1\rho_1 + a_2\rho_2 + \cdot \cdot \cdot \cdot \cdot$$

converges absolutely.

For, let a'_n, ρ'_n be the absolute values of a_n, ρ_n respectively, H a positive quantity greater than any of the quantities ρ'_n, and form the series

$$a'_0\rho'_0 + a'_1\rho'_1 + a'_2\rho'_2 + \cdot \cdot \cdot \cdot \cdot$$

The terms of this series are less respectively than the terms of the convergent series

$$Ha'_0 + Ha'_1 + Ha'_2 + \cdots\cdots$$

and each series is made up exclusively of positive terms. Hence the first series converges and the series

$$a_0\rho_0 + a_1\rho_1 + a_2\rho_2 + \cdots\cdots$$

converges absolutely.

Examples. 1. The series

$$\frac{\sin x}{1^2} - \frac{\sin 3x}{3^2} + \frac{\sin 5x}{5^2} - \cdots\cdots$$

converges absolutely for all values of x. For the series

$$\frac{1}{1^2} - \frac{1}{3^2} + \frac{1}{5^2} - \cdots\cdots$$

converges absolutely and $\sin nx$ never exceeds unity numerically.

2. If $a_0 + a_1 + a_2 + \cdots\cdots$ and $b_1 + b_2 + \cdots\cdots$ are any two absolutely convergent series, the series

$$a_0 + a_1 \cos x + a_2 \cos 2x + \cdots\cdots$$

and

$$b_1 \sin x + b_2 \sin 2x + \cdots\cdots$$

converge absolutely.

3. Show that the series

$$e^{-x} \cos x + e^{-2x} \cos 2x + \cdots\cdots$$

converges absolutely for all positive values of x.

4. What can you say about the convergence of the series

$$1 + r \cos \theta + r^2 \cos 2\theta + \cdots\cdots \quad ?$$

18. *Convergence and Divergence of Power Series.* A series of ascending integral powers of x,

$$a_0 + a_1x + a_2x^2 + \cdots\cdots,$$

where the coefficients $a_0, a_1, a_2, \cdots\cdots$ are independent of x, is called a *power series.* Such a series may converge for all values of x, but it will in general converge for some values and diverge for others. *In the latter case the interval of convergence extends equal distances in each direction from the point $x = 0$, and the series con-*

verges absolutely for every point x lying within this interval, but not necessarily for the extremities of the interval.

The proof is as follows. Let x_0 be any value of x for which the terms of the power series $a_n x_0^n$ do not increase without limit; a'_n, x'_0, the absolute values respectively of a_n, x_0. Then $a'_n x'^n_0$ is less than some fixed positive quantity C, independent of n, for all values of n. For $x = x_0$, the power series may converge and it may diverge. — Let h be any value of x numerically less than x'_0; h' its numerical value. Then the power series converges absolutely for $x = h$. For

$$a'_n h'^n = a'_n x'^n_0 \left(\frac{h'}{x'_0}\right)^n < Cr^n,$$

where $r = h'/x'_0 < 1$. Hence the terms of the absolute value series

$$a'_0 + a'_1 h' + a'_2 h'^2 + \cdot \cdot \cdot \cdot \cdot$$

are less respectively than the terms of the convergent geometric series

$$C + Cr + Cr^2 + \cdot \cdot \cdot \cdot \cdot$$

and the series

$$a_0 + a_1 h + a_2 h^2 + \cdot \cdot \cdot \cdot \cdot$$

converges absolutely.

From this theorem it follows that if the power series converges for $x = x_0$, it converges absolutely for all values of x within an interval stretching from 0 to x_0 and reaching out to the same distance on the other side of the point $x = 0$; and if diverges for $x = x_1$, it diverges for all values of x lying outside of the interval from x_1 to $- x_1$. If now the series ever diverges, consider the positive values of x for which it diverges. They fill a region extending down to a point $x = r$, where r in general is greater than 0 and such that the series converges absolutely for all values of x numerically less than r; and this is what was to be proved.

A simpler proof of this theorem can be given for the special case that a_{n+1}/a_n approaches a limit, L, when $n = \infty$. For then

$$\underset{n=\infty}{\text{Lim}} \frac{u_{n+1}}{u_n} = \lim_{n=\infty} \frac{a_{n+1} x^{n+1}}{a_n x^n} = Lx,$$

or $t = Lx$. Hence when $L = 0$, the power series converges absolutely for all values of x (§ 15); while if $L \neq 0$, the series converges absolutely when x is numerically less than $1/L$, and diverges when x is numerically greater than $1/L$. This proves the proposition.

II. SERIES AS A MEANS OF COMPUTATION.

---

a) THE LOGARITHMIC SERIES.

19. One of the most important applications of infinite series in analysis, and the one that chiefly concerns us in this course, is that of computing the numerical value of a complicated analytic expression, for example, of a definite integral like

$$\int_0^1 e^{-x^2} dx ,$$

when the indefinite integral cannot be found. In fact, the values of the elementary transcendental functions, the logarithm, sine, cosine, etc., are computed most simply in this way. Let us see how a table of logarithms can be computed from an infinite series.

A series for the function $\log_e (1 + h)$ can be obtained as follows. Begin with the formula

$$\log (1 + h) = \int_0^h \frac{dx}{1 + x} .$$

The function $(1 + x)^{-1}$ can be represented by the geometric series:

$$\frac{1}{1 + x} = 1 - x + x^2 - x^3 + \cdots\cdots$$

Integrate each side of this equation between the limits 0 and h:

$$\int_0^h \frac{dx}{1 + x} = \int_0^h 1 \cdot dx - \int_0^h x dx + \int_0^h x^2 dx - \cdots\cdots$$

Evaluating these integrals we are led to the desired formula:

$$\log (1 + h) = h - \frac{h^2}{2} + \frac{h^3}{3} - \cdots\cdots \tag{8}$$

In deducing the above formula it has been assumed that the theorem that the integral of a sum of terms is equal to the sum of the integrals of the terms can be extended to an infinite series. Now an infinite series is not a sum, but the *limit* of a sum, and hence the extension of this theorem requires justification. v. §§ 39, 40.

Exercise. Obtain the formula

$$\tan^{-1} h = h - \frac{h^3}{3} + \frac{h^5}{5} - \cdots\cdots$$

Hence evaluate the series

$$1 - \frac{1}{3} + \frac{1}{5} - \cdots\cdots$$

20. In the examples of § 12 the value of series (8) was computed to three places of decimals for $h = \frac{1}{3}$ and $h = \frac{1}{2}$; and it thus appears that

$$\log 1\tfrac{1}{3} = .287\ (5), \qquad \log 1\tfrac{1}{2} = .405\ (5).$$

To find log 2 we could substitute in (8) the value $h = 1$:

$$\log 2 = 1 - \tfrac{1}{2} + \tfrac{1}{3} - \tfrac{1}{4} + \cdots\cdots$$

But this series is not well adapted to numerical computation.* In fact to get the value of log 2 correct to the third place of decimals, it would be necessary to take 1000 terms. A simple device however makes the computation easy. Write

$$2 = \tfrac{4}{3} \cdot \tfrac{3}{2}$$

and then take the logarithm of each side:

$$\log 2 = \log \tfrac{4}{3} + \log \tfrac{3}{2}$$
$$= .287\ (5) + .405\ (5) = .693\ (0).$$

Hence, to three places, $\log 2 = .693$.

Next, to find log 5. Here the series must be applied in still a different way, for if $1 + h$ be set equal to 5, $h = 4$, and the series does not converge. We therefore set

$$5 = 4 + 1 = 4\ (1 + \tfrac{1}{4}),$$
$$\log 5 = 2 \log 2 + \log 1\tfrac{1}{4}$$
$$= 1.386\ (0) + .223\ (2) = 1.609\ (2),$$

where $\log 1\frac{1}{4}$ is computed directly from formula (8).

From the values of log 2 and log 5, log 10 can at once be found.

$$\log 10 = \log 2 + \log 5 = .693\ (0) + 1.609\ (2) = 2.302\ (2)$$

or to 3 places,

$$\log 10 = 2.302.$$

This latter logarithm is of great importance, for its value must be known in order to compute the denary logarithm from the natural

* The formula is nevertheless useful as showing the value of a familiar series, (6). We could not find by direct computation the value of this series to, say, seven places, because the work would be too long.

logarithm. By the formula for the transformation of logarithms from the base e to the base b,

$$\log_b A = \frac{\log_e A}{\log_e b},$$

we have

$$\log_{10} A = \frac{\log_e A}{\log_e 10}.$$

Hence for example

$$\log_{10} 2 = \frac{.693}{2.302} = .301.$$

Examples. Compute

$$\log 20, \qquad \log_{10} 20,$$

$$\log 9, \qquad \log_{10} 9,$$

$$\log 13, \qquad \log_{10} 13.$$

21. Series (8) is thus seen to serve its purpose well when only a few places of decimals are needed. Suppose however we wished to know log 2 correct to 7 places of decimals. Series (8) would then give less satisfactory results. In fact, it would require 16 terms of the series to yield log $1\frac{1}{3}$ to 7 places.

From (8) a new series can be deduced as follows. Let $h = -x$. Then (8) becomes

$$\log(1 - x) = -x - \frac{x^2}{2} - \frac{x^3}{3} - \cdots\cdots$$

Next replace h in (8) by x:

$$\log(1 + x) = +x - \frac{x^2}{2} + \frac{x^3}{3} - \cdots\cdots$$

Subtracting the former of these series from the latter and combining the logarithms we get the desired formula:

$$\log\frac{1+x}{1-x} = 2\left(x + \frac{x^3}{3} + \frac{x^5}{5} + \cdots\cdots\right) \qquad (9)$$

We have subtracted on the right hand side as if we had *sums*. We have not; we have *limits* of sums. This step will be justified in § 35.

We will now apply series (9) to the determination of log 2 to seven places. x must be so chosen that

$$\frac{1+x}{1-x} = 2, \qquad \text{i.e.} \qquad x = \tfrac{1}{3} \qquad \text{and}$$

$$\log\frac{1+\frac{1}{3}}{1-\frac{1}{3}} = 2\left(\frac{1}{3} + \frac{1}{3}\,\frac{1}{3^3} + \frac{1}{5}\,\frac{1}{3^5} + \frac{1}{7}\,\frac{1}{3^7} + \cdots\cdots\right)$$

The advantage of this series over (8) is twofold: first, it suffices to compute the value of the series for one value of x, $x = \frac{1}{3}$, and second, the series converges more rapidly than (8) for a given value of x, since only the odd powers of x enter.

$(\frac{1}{3})$	$= .333$	333	33	$(\frac{1}{3})$	$= .333$	333	33
$(\frac{1}{3})^3$	$= .037$	037	04	$\frac{1}{3}\cdot(\frac{1}{3})^3$	$= .012$	345	68
$(\frac{1}{3})^5$	$= .004$	115	23	$\frac{1}{5}\cdot(\frac{1}{3})^5$	$= .000$	823	05
$(\frac{1}{3})^7$	$= .000$	457	25	$\frac{1}{7}\cdot(\frac{1}{3})^7$	$= .000$	065	32
$(\frac{1}{3})^9$	$= .000$	050	81	$\frac{1}{9}\cdot(\frac{1}{3})^9$	$= .000$	005	65
$(\frac{1}{3})^{11}$	$= .000$	005	65	$\frac{1}{11}\cdot(\frac{1}{3})^{11}$	$= .000$	000	51
$(\frac{1}{3})^{13}$	$= .000$	000	63	$\frac{1}{13}\cdot(\frac{1}{3})^{13}$	$= .000$	000	05
$(\frac{1}{3})^{15}$	$= .000$	000	07	$\frac{1}{15}\cdot(\frac{1}{3})^{15}$	$= .000$	000	00
					.346	573	59

The term $\frac{1}{15}(\frac{1}{3})^{15}$ has no effect on the eighth decimal place. But this is not enough to justify us in stopping here. We must show that the *remainder* of the series from this point on cannot influence this place either. Now the remainder is the series

$$\frac{1}{15}\,\frac{1}{3^{15}} + \frac{1}{17}\,\frac{1}{3^{17}} + \frac{1}{19}\,\frac{1}{3^{19}} + \cdots\cdots$$

$$= \frac{1}{15}\,\frac{1}{3^{15}}\left[1 + \frac{15}{17}\,\frac{1}{3^2} + \frac{15}{19}\,\frac{1}{3^4} + \cdots\cdots\right]$$

The value of the series in brackets cannot be readily determined; nor is that necessary, for it is obviously less than the value of the series obtained from it by discarding the coefficients $\frac{15}{17}$, $\frac{15}{19}$, etc., i. e. than the geometric series

$$1 + \frac{1}{3^2} + \frac{1}{3^4} + \cdots\cdots = \frac{1}{1 - \frac{1}{9}} = \frac{9}{8}$$

and hence the remainder in question is less than

$$\frac{1}{15}\,\frac{1}{3^{15}}\,\frac{9}{8},$$

and so does not affect the eighth place.

We obtain then finally for log 2 the value

$$2 \times .346\ \ 573\ \ 5(9) = .693\ \ 147\ \ 1(8)$$

or to seven places

$$\log 2 \doteq .693\ \ 147\ \ 2.$$

Examples. Show that

$$\log 1\tfrac{1}{4} = .223 \quad 143 \quad (4)$$

$$\log 5 = 1.609 \quad 437 \quad (8).$$

Compute log 2 by aid of the formula

$$\log 2 = -\log \tfrac{1}{2} = -\log \tfrac{2}{3} - \log \tfrac{3}{4}.$$

Knowing log 2 and log 5 we can find log 10:

$$\log 10 = 2.302 \quad 585.$$

Example. Compute

$$\log_{10} 2, \qquad \log_{10} 9$$

to six places.

Series (9) is thus seen to be well adapted to the computation of logarithms. If y denote any positive number and x be so determined that

$$\frac{1+x}{1-x} = y, \quad \text{i. e.} \quad x = \frac{y-1}{y+1},$$

then x always lies between -1 and $+1$ and series (9) converges towards the value $\log y$. For values of y numerically large the convergence will be less rapid and devices similar to those above explained must be used to get the required result.

In the actual computation of a table, not all the values tabulated are computed directly from the series. A few values are computed in this way and the others are found by ingenious devices.

b) THE BINOMIAL SERIES.

22. In elementary algebra the Binomial Theorem for a positive integral exponent:

$$(a+b)^m = a^m + m a^{m-1} b + \frac{m(m-1)}{1 \cdot 2} a^{m-2} b^2 + \cdots \cdots \qquad \text{(to } m+1 \text{ terms)}$$

is established.

Consider the series

$$1 + \mu x + \frac{\mu(\mu-1)}{1 \cdot 2} x^2 + \frac{\mu(\mu-1)(\mu-2)}{1 \cdot 2 \cdot 3} x^3 + \cdots \cdots$$

If μ is a positive integer, this series breaks off with $\mu + 1$ terms, for then, from this point on, each numerator contains 0 as a factor. Thus if $\mu = 2$, we have

$$1 + 2x + \frac{2 \cdot 1}{1 \cdot 2} x^2 + \frac{2 \cdot 1 \cdot 0}{1 \cdot 2 \cdot 3} x^3 + \text{etc. (subsequent terms all 0)},$$

or simply $1 + 2x + x^2$. In this case the series is seen by comparison with the binomial formula ($a = 1$, $b = x$, $m = \mu$) to have the value $(1+x)^\mu$:

$$(1+x)^\mu = 1 + \mu x + \frac{\mu(\mu-1)}{1\cdot 2}x^2 + \frac{\mu(\mu-1)(\mu-2)}{1\cdot 2\cdot 3}x^3 + \cdots\cdots$$

If however μ is any number not a positive integer (negative number, fraction, etc.) the series never breaks off, i.e. it becomes an infinite series. Let us see for what values of x it converges, for only for such values will it have a meaning. The general term of the series is

$$\frac{\mu(\mu-1)(\mu-2)\cdots\cdots(\mu-n+1)}{1\quad 2\quad 3\cdots\cdots\cdots n}x^n$$

Hence

$$\frac{u_{n+1}}{u_n} = \frac{\dfrac{\mu(\mu-1)\cdots\cdots(\mu-n+1)(\mu-n)}{1\cdot 2\cdot\cdots\cdots n\cdot(n+1)}x^{n+1}}{\dfrac{\mu(\mu-1)\cdots\cdots(\mu-n+1)}{1\cdot 2\cdot\cdots\cdots n}x^n}$$

$$= \frac{\mu-n}{n+1}x = -\frac{1-\mu/n}{1+1/n}x$$

and

$$\lim_{n=\infty}\frac{u_{n+1}}{u_n} = -x.$$

Consequently the series converges for all values of x numerically less than unity. (§ 15.) For the values $x = 1, -1$ special investigation is necessary, which we will not go into here.

Divergent −1 0 1 Divergent
Convergent

We may note in passing that when $0 < x < 1$ the series finally becomes an alternating series, a fact that is useful when the series is used for computation.

Toward *what* value does the series converge when x lies between -1 and $+1$? The answer to this question is as follows: *For all values of x for which the binomial series converges, its value is* $(1+x)^\mu$:

$$(1+x)^\mu = 1 + \mu x + \frac{\mu(\mu-1)}{1\cdot 2}x^2 + \cdots\cdots \tag{10}$$

The proof of this theorem will not be considered here (v. Chap. III). Let us first see whether the series is of any value for the purposes of computation.

Example I. Let it be required to compute $\sqrt[3]{35}$ correct to five places.

We must throw the radicand into a form adapted to computation by the series. We do this as follows. Since $2^5 = 32$ we write

$$35 = 32 + 3 = 2^5\,(1 + \tfrac{3}{32}),$$
$$\sqrt[5]{35} = 2 \cdot (1 + \tfrac{3}{32})^{\frac{1}{5}}.$$

The second factor can be computed by aid of the series.

$$\mu = \tfrac{1}{5}, \quad x = \tfrac{3}{32},$$

$$(1 + \tfrac{3}{32})^{\frac{1}{5}} = 1 + \tfrac{1}{5}\,\tfrac{3}{32} + \frac{\frac{1}{5}\cdot\frac{-4}{5}}{1\cdot 2}\,(\tfrac{3}{32})^2 + \frac{\frac{1}{5}\cdot\frac{-4}{5}\cdot\frac{-9}{5}}{1\cdot 2\cdot 3}\,(\tfrac{3}{32})^3 + \cdots\cdots$$
$$= 1 + .018\ 750 - .000\ 703 + .000\ 010 - .000\ 003$$
$$= 1.018\ 08(4)$$

and
$$\sqrt[5]{35} = 2.036\ 17\,.$$

Exercise. Show that in the above computation we are justified in breaking off, as we did, with the fifth term.

Example II. Find $\sqrt[3]{15}$ to five places.

Here we have a choice between the expressions

$$15 = \ \ 8 + \ \ 7 = 2^3\,(1 + \tfrac{7}{8})$$

and

$$15 = 27 - 12 = 3^3\,(1 - \tfrac{4}{9})$$

In the first case $(1 + \frac{7}{8})^{\frac{1}{3}}$, in the second $(1 - \frac{4}{9})^{\frac{1}{3}}$ would be computed by aid of the series. In practice however there is no question as to which expression to use, for the second series converges more rapidly than the first.

Examples. 1. Complete the computation of $\sqrt[3]{15}$.

2. Show that $\sqrt[3]{9} = 2.080\ 09$ and $\sqrt[7]{2000} = 2.961\ 94$.

3. Compute $\sqrt{2}$ first by letting $\mu = -\frac{1}{2}$, $x = -\frac{1}{2}$; then by writing $2 = \frac{9}{4}\cdot\frac{8}{9}$.

4. Find $\sqrt[3]{2}$ to five places by any method.

5. Obtain from (10) the following formulas:

$$\frac{1}{1+x} = 1 - x + x^2 - x^3 + \cdots\cdots$$

$$\frac{1}{(1+x)^2} = 1 - 2x + 3x^2 - 4x^3 + \cdots\cdots$$

$$\frac{1}{\sqrt{1-x^2}} = 1 + \frac{1}{2}\,x^2 + \frac{1\cdot 3}{2\cdot 4}\,x^4 + \frac{1\cdot 3\cdot 5}{2\cdot 4\cdot 6}\,x^6 + \cdots\cdots$$

$$\sqrt{1-x^2} = 1 - \frac{1}{2}\,x^2 - \frac{1}{2\cdot 4}\,x^4 - \frac{1\cdot 3}{2\cdot 4\cdot 6}\,x^6 - \cdots\cdots$$

23. *Series for* $\sin^{-1}h$ *and* $\tan^{-1}h$. *The Computation of* π. The method set forth in § 19 is applicable to the representation of $\sin^{-1}h$ and $\tan^{-1}h$ (v. Exercise, § 19) by series.

$$\sin^{-1}h = \int_0^h \frac{dx}{\sqrt{1-x^2}} = h + \frac{1}{2}\frac{h^3}{3} + \frac{1\cdot 3}{2\cdot 4}\frac{h^5}{5} + \cdots\cdots \tag{11}$$

$$\tan^{-1}h = h - \frac{h^3}{3} + \frac{h^5}{5} - \cdots\cdots \tag{12}$$

From these series the value of π can be computed. If in series (12) we set $h=1$, we get the equation:

$$\frac{\pi}{4} = 1 - \frac{1}{3} + \frac{1}{5} - \frac{1}{7} + \cdots\cdots$$

This series, like series (6), is not well adapted to computation. A better series is obtained by putting $h = \frac{1}{2}$ in series (11):

$$\frac{\pi}{6} = \frac{1}{2} + \frac{1}{2}\cdot\frac{1}{3}\left(\frac{1}{2}\right)^3 + \frac{1\cdot 3}{2\cdot 4}\cdot\frac{1}{5}\left(\frac{1}{2}\right)^5 + \cdots\cdots$$

This series yields readily three or four places of decimals; but if greater accuracy is desired, more elaborate methods are necessary. (v. Jordan, *Cours d'Analyse*, Vol. I, § 262; 1893).

Exercise. If the radius of the Earth were exactly 4000 miles, to how many places of decimals would you need to know π in order to compute the circumference correct to one inch? Determine π to this number of places by Jordan's method.

24. *The Length of the Arc of an Ellipse.* Let the equation of the ellipse be given in the form:

$$x = a\sin\phi, \qquad y = b\cos\phi.$$

Then the length of the arc, measured from the end of the minor axis, will be

$$s = a\int_0^\phi \sqrt{1-e^2\sin^2\phi}\; d\phi,$$

where $(a^2-b^2)/a^2 = e^2 < 1$. The integral that here presents itself is known as an Elliptic Integral and its value cannot be found in the usual way, since the indefinite integral cannot be expressed in terms of the elementary functions. Its value can however be obtained by the aid of infinite series. The substitution of $e\sin\phi$ for x in the last example of § 22 gives the formula

$$\sqrt{1-e^2\sin^2\phi} = 1 - \frac{1}{2}e^2\sin^2\phi - \frac{1}{2\cdot 4}e^4\sin^4\phi - \cdots\cdots$$

Hence (v. § 40)

$$s = a\left[\phi - \frac{1}{2}e^2\int_0^\phi \sin^2\phi\, d\phi - \frac{1}{2\cdot 4}e^4\int_0^\phi \sin^4\phi\, d\phi \cdots\cdots\right]$$

These integrals can be evaluated by the aid of the formulas of IV of Peirce's *Short Table of Integrals.* In particular, the length of a quadrant S will be found by putting $\phi = \frac{1}{2}\pi$ and using the formula (No. 240 of the *Tables*)

$$\int_0^{\frac{\pi}{2}} \sin^n\phi\, d\phi = \frac{1\cdot 3\cdot 5\cdots\cdots(n-1)}{2\cdot 4\cdot 6\cdots\cdots n}\,\frac{\pi}{2},\quad n, \text{ an even integer.}$$

The elliptic integral then becomes the integral known as the Complete Elliptic Integral of the Second Kind; it is denoted by E:

$$E = \int_0^{\frac{\pi}{2}} \sqrt{1 - e^2\sin^2\phi}\; d\phi\,.$$

$$= \frac{\pi}{2}\left[1 - \left(\frac{1}{2}\right)^2 e^2 - \left(\frac{1\cdot 3}{2\cdot 4}\right)^2\frac{e^4}{3} - \left(\frac{1\cdot 3\cdot 5}{2\cdot 4\cdot 6}\right)^2\frac{e^6}{5}\cdots\cdots\right]$$

(No. 248 of the *Tables*). Hence

$$S = aE\,.$$

If $e = 0$ the ellipse reduces to a circle and $S = \frac{1}{2}\pi a$.

Examples. 1. Compute the perimeter of an ellipse whose major axis is twice as long as the minor axis, correct to one tenth of one percent.

2. A tomato can from which the top and bottom have been removed is bent into the shape of an elliptic cylinder, one axis of which is twice as long as the other. Find what size to make the new top and bottom. If the original can held a quart, how much will the new can hold?

25. *The Period of Oscillation of a Pendulum.* It is shown in Mechanics (v. Byerly's *Int. Cal.*, Chap. XVI) that the time of a complete oscillation of a pendulum of length l is given by the formula

$$T = 4K\sqrt{\frac{l}{g}},\qquad K = \int_0^{\frac{\pi}{2}}\frac{d\phi}{\sqrt{1 - k^2\sin^2\phi}},\qquad k = \sin\frac{a}{2},$$

where a denotes the initial inclination of the pendulum to the vertical. K is known as the Complete Elliptic Integral of the First Kind and its value is computed as follows. The substitution of $k\sin\phi$ for x in the series for $(1 - x^2)^{-\frac{1}{2}}$ gives the formula (v. *Exs.*, § 22).

$$\frac{1}{\sqrt{1 - k^2\sin^2\phi}} = 1 + \frac{1}{2}k^2\sin^2\phi + \frac{1\cdot 3}{2\cdot 4}k^4\sin^4\phi + \cdots\cdots$$

Integrating and reducing as in § 24, we obtain the formula

$$K = \int_0^{\frac{\pi}{2}} \frac{d\phi}{\sqrt{1 - k^2 \sin^2 \phi}} = \frac{\pi}{2}\left[1 + \left(\frac{1}{2}\right)^2 k^2 + \left(\frac{1 \cdot 3}{2 \cdot 4}\right)^2 k^4 + \cdots\cdots\right]$$

If the angle through which the pendulum oscillates is small, an approximation for T sufficiently accurate for most purposes will be obtained by putting $k = 0$. Then $K = \frac{1}{2}\pi$ and

$$T = 2\pi \sqrt{\frac{l}{g}},$$

the usual pendulum formula.

Exercise. Show that if $\alpha < 5°$, this approximation is correct to less than one tenth of one percent.

c) APPROXIMATE FORMULAS IN APPLIED MATHEMATICS.

26. It is often possible to replace a complicated formula in applied mathematics by a simpler one which is still correct within the limits of error of the observations.*

The Coefficient of Expansion. By the coefficient of linear expansion of a solid is meant the ratio

$$\alpha = \frac{l' - l}{l},$$

where l is the length of a piece of the substance at temperature $t°$, l' the length at temperature $t'°$. The coefficient of cubical expansion is defined similarly as

$$\beta = \frac{V' - V}{V},$$

where V, V' stand for the volumes at temperature $t°$, $t'°$ respectively. Then

$$\frac{V' - V}{V} = \frac{l'^3 - l^3}{l^3},$$

as is at once clear if we consider a cube of the substance, the length of an edge being l at $t°$. The accurate expression for α in terms of β is as follows.

$$\frac{l'}{l} = 1 + \alpha = \sqrt[3]{1 + \beta},$$

$$\alpha = \sqrt[3]{1 + \beta} - 1 = \tfrac{1}{3}\beta - \tfrac{1}{9}\beta^2 + \cdots\cdots$$

* See Kohlrausch, *Physical Measurements*, §§ 1-6.

Since β is small, — usually less than .0001, — the error made by neglecting all terms of the series subsequent to the first is less than the errors of observation and hence we may assume without any loss of accuracy that

$$\alpha = \tfrac{1}{3}\beta, \qquad \beta = 3\alpha.$$

Double Weighing. Show that if the apparent weight of a body when placed in one scale pan is p_1, when placed in the other scale pan, p_2 (the difference being due to a slight inequality in the lengths of the arms of the balance), the true weight p is given with sufficient accuracy by the formula:

$$p = \tfrac{1}{2}(p_1 + p_2).$$

27. *Errors of Observation.* In an experimental determination of a physical magnitude it is important to know what effect an error in an observed value will have on the final result. For example, let it be required to determine the radius of a capillary tube by measuring the length of a column of mercury contained in the tube, and weighing the mercury. From the formula

$$w = \pi r^2 l \rho,$$

where w denotes the weight of the mercury in grammes, l the length of the column in centimetres, ρ the density of the mercury ($= 13.6$), and r the radius of the tube, we get

$$r = \sqrt{\frac{w}{\pi \rho l}} = .1530 \sqrt{\frac{w}{l}}.$$

Now the principal error in determining r arises from the error in observing l. Let l be the true value, $l' = l + e$ the observed value of the length of the column; r the true value, $r' = r + E$ the computed value of the radius. Then E is the error in the result arising from the error of observation e, the error in observing w being assumed negligible. Hence

$$E = .153\sqrt{\frac{w}{l'}} - .153\sqrt{\frac{w}{l}} = .153\sqrt{\frac{w}{l}}\left(\left(1 + \frac{e}{l}\right)^{-\frac{1}{2}} - 1\right)$$

$$= r\left(-\frac{1}{2}\frac{e}{l} + \frac{3}{8}\frac{e^2}{l^2}\cdots\cdots\right)$$

Since e is small we get a result sufficiently accurate by taking only the first term; and hence, approximately,

$$E = -\tfrac{1}{2} r \cdot \frac{1}{l} \cdot e.$$

Thus for a given error in observing l, the error in the computed value of r is inversely proportional to the length of the column of mercury used, — a result not *a priori* obvious, for r itself is inversely proportioned only to $\sqrt{l}$.

Exercise. An engineer surveys a field, using a chain that is incorrect by one tenth of one percent of its length. Show that the error thus arising in the determination of the area of the field will be two tenths of one percent of the area.

28. *Pendulum Problems.* A clock regulated by a pendulum is located at a point (A) on the earth's surface. If it is carried to a neighboring point (B), h feet above the level of (A), show that it will lose $\frac{1}{244}h$ seconds a day, i. e. one second for every 244 feet of elevation.

The number of seconds N that the clock registers in 24 hours is inversely proportional to the period T of the oscillation of the pendulum. Hence (cf. §25)

$$\frac{N'}{N}=\frac{T}{T'}=\sqrt{\frac{g'}{g}},$$

where the unprimed letters refer to the location (A), the primed letters to (B). If the clock was keeping true time at (A), then $N=86{,}400$.

$$\frac{g'}{g}=\frac{R^2}{(R+h)^2},$$

where R denotes the length of the radius of the earth. (Cf. Byerly's *Diff. Cal.*, §117.) Hence

$$N-N'=N\left(1-\sqrt{\frac{g'}{g}}\right)=N\frac{h}{R+h}$$

$$=N\frac{h}{R}-N\frac{h^2}{R^2}+N\frac{h^3}{R^3}=\cdots\cdots$$

If h does not exceed 5 miles, $h/R<.001$. $h^2/R^2<.000\,001$, and the first term of the series gives $N-N'$ correct to seconds:

$$N-N'=\tfrac{1}{244}h.$$

Examples. 1. The summit of Mt. Washington is 6226 feet above the sea level. How many seconds a day will a clock lose that keeps accurate time in Boston Harbor, if carried to the summit of the Mountain?

2. A pendulum that beats seconds on the surface of the earth is observed to gain one second an hour when carried to the bottom of a mine. How deep is the mine?

29. *Exercises.* 1. Show that the correction for expansion and contraction due to heat and cold is given by the formula

$$n = 43{,}200\, a\, t,$$

where a denotes the coefficient of linear expansion, t the rise in temperature, and n the number of seconds lost in a day.

For brass, $a = .000\,019$, t being measured in degrees centigrade. Thus for a brass pendulum $n = .82\,t$, and a rise in temperature of 5° causes the clock to lose a little over 4 seconds a day.

2. A man is standing on the deck of a ship and his eyes are h ft. above the sea level. If D denotes the shortest distance of a ship away whose masts and rigging he can see, but whose hull is invisible to him, h_1 the height, measured in feet, to which the hull rises out of the water, show that, if refraction can be neglected,

$$D = 1.23\,(\sqrt{h} + \sqrt{h_1}) \text{ miles.}$$

If $h = h_1 = 16$ ft., $D = 10$ miles (nearly).

3. Show that an arc of a great circle of the earth, 2½ miles long, recedes 1 foot from its chord.

4. Assuming that the sun's parallax is 8″.76, prove that the distance of the sun from the earth is about 94 million miles.

5. Show that in levelling the correction for the curvature of the earth is 8 in. for one mile. How much is it for two miles?

6. The weights of an astronomical clock exert, through faulty construction of the clock, a greater propelling force when the clock has just been wound up than when it has nearly run down, and thus increase the amplitude of the pendulum from 2° to 2° 4′ on each side of the vertical. Show that if the clock keeps correct time when it has nearly run down, it will lose at the rate of about .4 of a second a day when it has just been wound up.

7. Two nearly equal, but unknown resistances, A and B, form two arms of a Wheatstone's Bridge. A standard box of coils and a resistance x to be measured form the other two arms. A balance is obtained when the standard rheostat has a resistance of r ohms. When however A and B are interchanged, a balance is obtained when the resistance of the rheostat is r' ohms. Show that, approximately,

$$x = \tfrac{1}{2}(r + r').$$

8. The focal length f of a lens is given by the formula

$$\frac{1}{f} = \frac{1}{p_1} + \frac{1}{p_2},$$

where p_1 and p_2 denote two conjugate focal distances. Obtain a simpler approximate formula for f that will answer when p_1 and p_2 are nearly equal.

9. "A ranchman 6 feet 7 inches tall, standing on a level plain, agrees to buy at $7 an acre all the land in sight. How much must he pay? Given 640 acres make a square mile." Admission Exam. in Sol. Geom., June, 1895.

Show that if the candidate had assumed the altitude of the zone in sight to be equal to the height of the ranchman's eyes above the ground and had made no other error in his solution, his answer would have been 4 cents too small.

10. Show that for small values of h the following equations are approximately correct (h may be either positive or negative)

$$(1+h)^m = 1 + mh.$$

Hence $(1+h)^2 = 1 + 2h;$ $\qquad \sqrt{1+h} = 1 + \tfrac{1}{2}h;$

$$\frac{1}{1+h} = 1 - h; \qquad \frac{1}{(1+h)^2} = 1 - 2h;$$

$$\frac{1}{\sqrt{1+h}} = 1 - \tfrac{1}{2}h.$$

If $h, k, l, p, \cdots\cdots$ are all numerically small, then, approximately,

$$(1+h)(1+k)(1+l)\cdots\cdots = 1 + h + k + l + \cdots\cdots,$$

$$\frac{(1+h)(1+k)\cdots\cdots}{(1+l)(1+p)\cdots\cdots} = 1 + h + k\cdots\cdots - l - p - \cdots\cdots$$

III. TAYLOR'S THEOREM.

30. It is not the object of this chapter to prove Taylor's Theorem, since this is done satisfactorily in any good treatise on the Differential Calculus; but to indicate its bearing on the subject under consideration and to point out a few of its most important applications.

It is remarkable that this fundamental theorem in infinite series admits a simple and rigorous proof of an entirely elementary nature. Rolle's Theorem, on which Taylor's Theorem depends, and the Law of the Mean lie at the very foundation of the differential calculus. From Rolle's Theorem follows at once the theorem contained in the equation

$$f(x_0+h)=f(x_0)+f'(x_0)h+f''(x_0)\frac{h^2}{2!}+\cdots+f^{(n)}(x_0+\theta h)\frac{h^n}{n!}, \quad (13)$$

$$0<\theta<1.$$

This latter theorem is frequently referred to as *Taylor's Theorem with the Remainder* $\left[R_n = f^{(n)}(x_0+\theta h)\frac{h^n}{n!}\right]$. It includes the Law of the Mean

$$f(x_0+h)-f(x_0)=hf'(x_0+\theta h) \quad (14)$$

as a special case and thus affords a proof of that Law. If in (13), when n increases indefinitely, R_n converges towards 0 as its limit, the series on the right hand side of (13) becomes an infinite power series, representing the function $f(x_0+h)$ throughout a certain region about the point x_0:

$$f(x_0+h)=f(x_0)+f'(x_0)h+f''(x_0)\frac{h^2}{2!}+\cdots\cdots \quad (15)$$

This formula is known as *Taylor's Theorem* and the series as *Taylor's Series*.

The value x_0 is an arbitrary value of x which, once chosen, is held fast. The variable x is then written as x_0+h. The object of this is as follows. It is desired to obtain a simple representation of the function $f(x)$ in terms of known elements, for the purpose of computing the value of the function or studying its properties. One of the simplest of such forms is a power series with known coefficients.

Now it is usually impossible to represent $f(x)$ by one and the same power series for all values of x, and even when this is possible, the series will not converge rapidly enough for large values of the argument to be of use in computation. Consequently we confine our attention to a limited domain of values, choose an x_0 in the midst of this domain, and replace the independent variable x by h, where

$$x = x_0 + h, \qquad h = x - x_0.$$

The values of x for the domain in question may not be small, but the values of h will be, $h = 0$ corresponding to $x = x_0$. If x_0 is so chosen that $f(x_0), f'(x_0), f''(x_0), \ldots\ldots$ *ad inf.* are all finite, then the value of $f(x)$ for values of x near to x_0, i. e. for values of h numerically small, will usually* be given by Taylor's Theorem.

An example will aid in making clear the above general statements. Let

$$f(x) = \log x.$$

Then it is at once clear that $f(x)$ *cannot* be developed by Taylor's Theorem for $x_0 = 0$, for $f(0) = \log 0 = -\infty$. It is just at this point that the freedom that we have in the choice of x_0 stands us in good stead; for if we take x_0 greater than 0, then $f(x_0)$, $f'(x_0)$, $f''(x_0), \ldots\ldots$ will all be finite and $f(x_0 + h)$ can be developed by Taylor's Theorem, the series converging for all values of h lying between x_0 and $-x_0$. The proof is given for $x_0 = 1$ in the *Diff. Cal.*, § 130. Thus we have a second proof of the development of $\log(1 + h)$, (formula (8) of § 19).

31. *Two Applications of Taylor's Theorem with the Remainder, (13).* This theorem, it will be observed, is not a theorem in infinite series. Any function whose first n derivatives are continuous can be expressed in the form (13), while the expression in the form (15) requires the proof of the possibility of passing to the limit when $n = \infty$.

Thus (13) is a more general theorem than (15) and it avoids the necessity of a proof of convergence.† It is because of the applications that (13) and (15) have in common, that it seemed desirable to treat some applications of (13) here.

* Exceptions to this rule, though possible, are extremely rare in ordinary practice.

† It is desirable that (13) should be applied much more freely than has hitherto been the custom in works on the Infinitesimal Calculus, both because it affords a simple means of proof in a vast variety of cases and because many proofs usually given by the aid of (15) can be simplified or rendered rigorous by the aid of (13). The applications given in this section are cases in point.

First Application: Maxima, Minima and Points of Inflection; Curvature. Let it be required to study the function $f(x)$ in the neighborhood of the point $x = x_0$.

$$f(x_0 + h) = f(x_0) + f'(x_0)\,h + \tfrac{1}{2} f''(x_0 + \theta h)\,h^2.$$

Plot the function as a curve: *

$$y_1 = f(x) = f(x_0 + h),$$

and plot the curve

$$y_2 = f(x_0) + f'(x_0)\,h = f(x_0) + f'(x_0)\,(x - x_0).$$

The latter curve is a right line. Consider the difference of the ordinates, y_1 and y_2

$$y_1 - y_2 = \tfrac{1}{2} f''(x_0 + \theta h)\,h^2.$$

Hence it appears that $y_1 - y_2$ is an infinitesimal of the second order. This property characterizes the line in question as the tangent to the curve in the point x_0, and thus we get a new proof that the equation of the tangent is

$$y = f(x_0) + f'(x_0)\,(x - x_0).$$

Next, suppose

$$f'(x_0) = 0, \quad \cdots\cdots \quad f^{(2n-1)}(x_0) = 0, \quad f^{(2n)}(x_0) > 0.$$

Then
$$f(x_0 + h) = f(x_0) + f^{(2n)}(x_0 + \theta h)\,\frac{h^{2n}}{(2n)!}.$$

The equation of the tangent is now

$$y_2 = f(x_0)$$

and
$$y_1 - y_2 = f^{(2n)}(x_0 + \theta h)\,\frac{h^{2n}}{(2n)!}$$

$f^{(2n)}(x)$ will in general be continuous near the point $x = x_0$ and it is positive at this point; it will therefore be positive in the neighborhood of this point and hence

$$y_1 - y_2 > 0$$

both for positive and for negative values of h, i.e. the curve lies above its tangent and has therefore a minimum at the point $x = x_0$.

Similarly it can be shown that if $f^{(2n)}(x_0) < 0$, all the earlier derivatives vanishing, $f(x)$ has a maximum in the point x_0.

Lastly, let

$$f'(x_0) = 0, \quad \cdots\cdots \quad f^{(2n)}(x_0) = 0, \quad f^{(2n+1)}(x_0) \neq 0.$$

* The student should illustrate each case in this § by a figure.

Then $$y_1 - y_2 = f^{(2n+1)}(x_0 + \theta h) \cdot \frac{h^{2n+1}}{(2n+1)!}.$$

$f^{(2n+1)}(x)$ will in general be continuous near $x = x_0$ and it will therefore preserve the same sign for small values of h, positive or negative; but h^{2n+1} changes sign with h. Hence the curve lies on opposite sides of its tangent on opposite sides of the point x_0 and this is then a point of inflection.

Exercises. 1. Show that the condition for a point of inflection not parallel to the x-axis is

$$f''(x_0) = 0, \quad \cdots\cdots \quad f^{(2n)}(x_0) = 0, \quad f^{(2n+1)}(x_0) \neq 0,$$

$f^{(2n+1)}(x)$ being continuous near $x = x_0$.

2. Show that a perpendicular drawn to the tangent from a point P' infinitely near to a point of inflection P is an infinitesimal of higher order than the second.

Curvature. The osculating circle was defined (*Diff. Cal.* § 90) as a circle tangent to the given curve at P and having its centre on the inner normal at a distance ρ (the radius of curvature) from P. We will now show that if a point P' be taken infinitely near to P and a perpendicular $P'M$ be dropped from P' on the tangent at P, cutting the osculating circle at P'', then $P'P''$ is in general an infinitesimal of the third order referred to the arc PP' as principal infinitesimal. Let P be taken as the origin of coördinates, the tangent at P being the axis of x and the inner normal the axis of y; and let the ordinate y be represented by the aid of (13). Here

$$x_0 = 0, \quad x = h, \quad f(0) = f'(0) = 0, \quad f''(0) > 0,$$

and $$y = \tfrac{1}{2} f''(0)\, x^2 + \tfrac{1}{6} f'''(\theta x)\, x^3.$$

The radius of curvature at P is

$$\rho = \frac{[1 + (D_x y)^2]^{\frac{3}{2}}}{D_x^{\,2} y} = \frac{1}{f''(0)}$$

and the equation of the osculating circle is

$$x^2 + (y - \rho)^2 = \rho.$$

Hence the lesser ordinate y' of this circle is given by the formula:*

$$y' = \rho - \sqrt{\rho^2 - x^2} = \rho - \rho\left(1 - \tfrac{1}{2}\frac{x^2}{\rho^2} - \tfrac{1}{8}\frac{x^4}{\rho^4} \cdots\cdots\right)$$

$$= \tfrac{1}{2}\frac{1}{\rho}x^2 + \tfrac{1}{8}\frac{1}{\rho^3}x^4 \cdots\cdots$$

* Instead of the infinite series, formula (13) might have been used here, with $n = 4$. But we happen to know in this case that the function can be developed by Taylor's Theorem (15).

and $$y - y' = x^3\left(\tfrac{1}{6}f'''(\theta x) - \tfrac{1}{8}\frac{1}{\rho^3}x \cdot \cdot \cdot \cdot \cdot \cdot\right).$$

From this result follows that $(y - y')/x^3$ approaches in general a finite limit different from 0, and hence that $y - y'$ is an infinitesimal of the *third* order, referred to $P'M = x$ as principal infinitesimal. But $P'M$ and PP' are of the same order. Hence the proposition.

Exercise. Show that for any other tangent circle $y - y'$ is an infinitesimal of the second order.

Second Application: Error of Observation. Let x denote the magnitude to be observed, $y = f(x)$ the magnitude to be computed from the observation. Then if x_0 be the true value of the observed magnitude, $x = x_0 + h$ the value determined by the observation, h will be the error in the observation, and the error H caused thereby in the result will be (*cf.* (14))

$$H = f(x_0 + h) - f(x_0) = f'(x_0 + \theta h)h.$$

In general $f'(x)$, will be a continuous function of x and thus the value of $f'(x_0 + \theta h)$ will be but slightly changed if $x_0 + \theta h$ is replaced by x. Hence, approximately,

$$H = f'(x)\,h$$

and this is the formula that gives the error in the result due to the error in the observation.

32. *The Principal Applications of Taylor's Theorem without the Remainder, i. e. Taylor's Series (15)* consist in showing that the fundamental elementary functions: e^x, $\sin x$, $\cos x$, $\log x$, x^μ, $\sin^{-1}x$, $\tan^{-1}x$ can be represented by a Taylor's Series, and in determining explicitly the coefficients in these series. It is shown in Ch. IX of the *Diff. Cal.* that these developments are as follows.*

$$e^x = 1 + x + \frac{x^2}{2!} + \frac{x^3}{3!} + \cdot \cdot \cdot \cdot \cdot$$

$$\sin x = x - \frac{x^3}{3!} + \frac{x^5}{5!} - \cdot \cdot \cdot \cdot \cdot$$

$$\cos x = 1 - \frac{x^2}{2!} + \frac{x^4}{4!} - \cdot \cdot \cdot \cdot \cdot$$

These developments hold for all values of x.

* The developments for $\sin^{-1}x$ and $\tan^{-1}x$ are to be sure obtained by integration; but the student will have no difficulty in obtaining them directly from Taylor's Theorem.

$$\log x = \log(1+h) = h - \frac{h^2}{2} + \frac{h^3}{3} - \cdots\cdots$$

$$x^\mu = (1+h)^\mu = 1 + \mu h + \frac{\mu(\mu-1)}{1\cdot 2}h^2 + \cdots\cdots$$

$$\sin^{-1}x = x + \frac{1}{2}\frac{x^3}{3} + \frac{1\cdot 3}{2\cdot 4}\frac{x^5}{5} + \cdots\cdots$$

$$\tan^{-1}x = x - \frac{x^3}{3} + \frac{x^5}{5} - \cdots\cdots$$

These developments hold for all values of h (or, in the case of the last two formulas, of x) numerically less than 1.

Exercise. Show that $\sin x$ can be developed about any point x_0 by Taylor's Theorem and that the series will converge for all values of h. Hence compute $\sin 46°$ correct to seconds.

33. As soon however as we pass beyond the simple functions and try to apply Taylor's Theorem, we encounter a difficulty that is usually insurmountable. In order namely to show that $f(x)$ can be expanded by Taylor's Theorem it is necessary to investigate the general expression for the n-th derivative, and this expression is usually extremely complicated. To avoid this difficulty recourse is had to more or less indirect methods of obtaining the expansion. For example, let it be required to evaluate

$$\int_0^1 \frac{e^x - e^{-x}}{x}\,dx.$$

The indefinite integral cannot be obtained and thus we are driven to develop the integrand into a series and integrate term by term. Now if we try to apply Taylor's Theorem to the function $(e^x - e^{-x})/x$, the successive derivatives soon become complicated. We can however proceed as follows:

$$e^x = 1 + x + \frac{x^2}{2!} + \frac{x^3}{3!} + \cdots\cdots,$$

$$e^{-x} = 1 - x + \frac{x^2}{2!} - \frac{x^3}{3!} + \cdots\cdots,$$

$$e^x - e^{-x} = 2\left(x + \frac{x^3}{3!} + \frac{x^5}{5!} + \cdots\cdots\right);$$

and hence, dividing through by x, we have

$$\frac{e^x - e^{-x}}{x} = 2\left(1 + \frac{x^2}{3!} + \frac{x^4}{5!} + \cdots\cdots\right),$$

$$\int_0^1 \frac{e^x - e^{-x}}{x} dx = 2\left(1 + \frac{1}{3 \cdot 3!} + \frac{1}{5 \cdot 5!} + \cdots\cdots\right) = 2.114\ 502 \cdot$$

Examples. Do the examples on p. 50 of the *Problems.*

General Method for the Expansion of a Function. To develop a function $f(x)$, made up in a simple manner out of the elementary functions, into a power series, the general method is the following. The fundamental elementary functions having been developed by Taylor's Theorem, § 32, we proceed to study some of the simplest operations that can be performed on series and thus, starting with the developments already obtained, pass to the developments desired.

IV. ALGEBRAIC TRANSFORMATIONS OF SERIES.

34. It has been pointed out repeatedly (§§ 19, 21, 24) that since an infinite series is not a sum, but a *limit* of a sum, processes applicable to a sum need not be applicable to a series; if applicable, this fact requires proof.

For example, the value of a sum is independent of the order in which the terms are added. Can this interchange in the order of the terms be extended to series? Let us see. Take the series

$$1 - \tfrac{1}{2} + \tfrac{1}{3} - \tfrac{1}{4} + \cdots\cdots \qquad (\alpha)$$

Its value is *less* than $1 - \frac{1}{2} + \frac{1}{3} = \frac{5}{6}$ (§ 12) Rearrange its terms as follows:

$$1 + \tfrac{1}{3} - \tfrac{1}{2} + \tfrac{1}{5} + \tfrac{1}{7} - \tfrac{1}{4} + \tfrac{1}{9} + \tfrac{1}{11} - \tfrac{1}{6} + \cdots\cdots \qquad (\beta)$$

The general formula for three successive terms is

$$\frac{1}{4k-3} + \frac{1}{4k-1} - \frac{1}{2k}$$

and if each pair of positive terms be enclosed in parentheses:

$$(1 + \tfrac{1}{3}) - \tfrac{1}{2} + (\tfrac{1}{5} + \tfrac{1}{7}) - \tfrac{1}{4} + (\tfrac{1}{9} + \tfrac{1}{11}) - \tfrac{1}{6} + \cdots\cdots \qquad (\gamma)$$

the result is an alternating series of the kind considered in (§ 11). For it is easy to verify the inequalities

$$\frac{1}{4k-3} + \frac{1}{4k-1} > \frac{1}{2k} > \frac{1}{4k+1} + \frac{1}{4k+3}.$$

Hence the series (γ) converges toward a value *greater* than $(1 + \frac{1}{3}) - \frac{1}{2} = \frac{5}{6}$. The sum of the first n terms of (β) differs from a properly chosen sum of terms of (γ) at most by the first term of a parenthesis, — a quantity that approaches 0 as its limit when $n = \infty$. Hence the series (β) and (γ) have the same value and the rearrangement of terms in (α) has thus led to a series (β) having a *different value* from (α).

In fact it is possible to rearrange the terms in (α) so that the new series will have an arbitrarily preassigned value, C. For, if C is positive, say 10 000, begin by adding from the positive terms

$$1 + \tfrac{1}{3} + \tfrac{1}{5} + \cdots\cdots$$

till enough have been taken so that their sum will just exceed C. This will always be possible, since this series of positive terms diverges. Then begin with the negative terms

$$-\tfrac{1}{2}-\tfrac{1}{4}-\tfrac{1}{6}\cdot\cdot\cdot\cdot\cdot\cdot$$

and add just enough to reduce the sum below C. As soon as this has been done, begin again with the positive terms and add just enough to bring the sum above C; and so on. The series thus obtained is the result of a rearrangement of the terms of (a) and its value is C.

In the same way it can be shown generally that if

$$u_0+u_1+u_2+\cdot\cdot\cdot\cdot\cdot\cdot$$

is any convergent series that is *not absolutely* convergent, its terms can be so rearranged that the new series will converge toward the pre-assigned value C. Because of this fact such series are often called *conditionally convergent*, Theorem 1 of § 35 justifying the denoting of absolutely convergent series as *unconditionally convergent*.

There is nothing paradoxical in this fact, if a correct view of the nature of an infinite series is entertained. For a rearrangement of terms means a replacement of the original variable s_n by a new variable s'_n, in general unequal to s_n, and there is no *a priori* reason why these two variables should approach the same limit.

The above example illustrates the impossibility of extending *a priori* to infinite series processes applicable to sums. Most of such processes are however capable of such extension *under proper restrictions*, and it is the object of this chapter to study such extension for some of the most fundamental processes.

35. Theorem 1. *In an absolutely convergent series the terms can be rearranged at pleasure without altering the value of the series.*

First, suppose all the terms to be positive and let

$$s_n=u_0+u_1+\cdot\cdot\cdot\cdot\cdot\cdot+u_{n-1}; \qquad \lim_{n=\infty} s_n=U.$$

After the rearrangement let

$$s'_{n'}=u'_0+u'_1+\cdot\cdot\cdot\cdot\cdot\cdot+u'_{n'-1}.$$

Then $s'_{n'}$ approaches the limit U when $n'=\infty$. For $s'_{n'}$ always increases as n' increases; but no matter how large n' be taken (and then held fast), n can (subsequently) be taken so large that s_n will include *all* the terms of $s'_{n'}$ and more too; therefore

$$s'_{n'}<s_n<U;$$

or, no matter how large n' be taken,

$$s'_{n'} < U.$$

Hence $s'_{n'}$ approaches a limit $U' \leqq U$.

We may now turn things about and regard the u-series as generated by a rearrangement of the terms of the u'-series, and the above reasoning shows that $U \leqq U'$; hence $U' = U$. *q. e. d.*

Exercise. The second step in the above proof was abbreviated by an ingenious device. Replace this device by a direct line of reasoning.

Secondly, let the series

$$u_0 + u_1 + u_2 + \cdots\cdots$$

be any absolutely convergent series and let

$$s_n = \sigma_m - \tau_p, \qquad \text{(Cf. § 14)}$$

$$U = V - W.$$

Let

$$u'_0 + u'_1 + u'_2 \cdots\cdots$$

be the series after the rearrangement and let

$$s'_{n'} = \sigma'_{m'} - \tau'_{p'},$$

$$U' = V' - W'.$$

But $V' = V$ and $W' = W$; hence $U' = U$.

Exercise. Find the value of the series

$$\frac{1}{2^1} + \frac{1}{2^3} - \frac{1}{2^2} + \frac{1}{2^5} + \frac{1}{2^7} - \frac{1}{2^4} + \frac{1}{2^9} + \frac{1}{2^{11}} - \frac{1}{2^6} + \cdots\cdots$$

THEOREM 2. *If*

$$U = u_0 + u_1 + \cdots\cdots$$

$$V = v_0 + v_1 + \cdots\cdots$$

are any two convergent series, they can be added term by term, or

$$U + V = u_0 + v_0 + u_1 + v_1 + u_2 + \cdots\cdots$$

If they are absolutely convergent, the third series will also be absolutely convergent and hence its terms can be rearranged at pleasure.

Let

$$s_n = u_0 + u_1 + \cdots\cdots + u_{n-1},$$

$$t_n = t_0 + t_1 + \cdots\cdots + t_{n-1}.$$

Then

$$s_n + t_n = (u_0 + v_0) + (u_1 + v_1) + \cdots\cdots + (u_{n-1} + v_{n-1}).$$

When $n = \infty$, the left hand side converges toward $U + V$; hence

$$U + V = (u_0 + v_0) + (u_1 + v_1) + \cdots\cdots$$

It remains to show that the parentheses may be dropped. This is shown in the same way as in the case which arose in § 34.

The proof of the second part of the theorem presents no difficulty and may be left to the student.

Exercise. Show that if

$$U = u_0 + u_1 + u_2 + \cdots\cdots$$

is any convergent series, c any number,

$$cU = cu_0 + cu_1 + cu_2 + \cdots\cdots$$

THEOREM 3. *If*

$$U = u_0 + u_1 + u_2 + \cdots\cdots$$
$$V = v_0 + v_1 + v_2 + \cdots\cdots$$

are any two absolutely convergent series, they can be multiplied together like sums; i. e. if each term in the first series be multiplied into each term in the second and the series of these products formed, this series will converge absolutely toward the limit UV. For example

$$UV = u_0v_0 + u_0v_1 + u_1v_0 + u_0v_2 + u_1v_1 + u_2v_0 + \cdots\cdots$$

This theorem does not hold for series that are not absolutely convergent.

Let

$$s_n = u_0 + u_1 + \cdots\cdots + u_{n-1},$$
$$t_n = v_0 + v_1 + \cdots\cdots + v_{n-1};$$

then

$$\lim_{n=\infty} s_n t_n = UV.$$

The terms of the product $s_n t_n$ are advantageously displayed in the following scheme. They are those terms contained in a square n terms on a side, cut out of the upper left hand corner of the scheme.

$$\begin{array}{l}
u_0v_0 + u_0v_1 + u_0v_2 + u_0v_3 + \cdots\cdots \\
u_1v_0 + u_1v_1 + u_1v_2 + u_1v_3 + \cdots\cdots \\
u_2v_0 + u_2v_1 + u_2v_2 + u_2v_3 + \cdots\cdots \\
u_3v_0 + u_3v_1 + u_3v_2 + u_3v_3 + \cdots\cdots \\
\cdot \quad \cdot \quad \cdot \quad \cdot \quad \cdot \quad \cdot \quad \cdot
\end{array}$$

The theorem asserts that if any series be formed by adding the terms of this scheme, each term appearing in this series once and only once, — for example, the terms that lie on the oblique lines, the successive lines being followed from top to bottom:

$$u_0 v_0 + u_0 v_1 + u_1 v_0 + u_0 v_2 + \cdots\cdots, \qquad (\alpha)$$

this series will converge absolutely toward the limit UV.

It is sufficient to show that *one* series formed in the prescribed way from the terms of the scheme, for example the series formed by following the successive boundaries of the squares from top to bottom and then from right to left, namely the series

$$u_0 v_0 + u_0 v_1 + u_1 v_1 + u_1 v_0 + u_0 v_2 + \cdots\cdots \qquad (\beta)$$

converges absolutely toward the limit UV. For any other series can then be generated by a rearrangement of the terms of this series.

Let S_N denote the sum of the first N terms in (β).

First suppose all the terms of the u-series and the v-series to be positive.* Then, if $n^2 \leqq N < (n+1)^2$,

$$s_n t_n \leqq S_N \leqq s_{n+1} t_{n+1}.$$

Hence
$$\lim_{N=\infty} S_N = UV.$$

Secondly, if the u-series and the v-series are any absolutely convergent series, form the series of absolute values

$$u'_0 + u'_1 + u'_2 + \cdots\cdots$$

$$v'_0 + v'_1 + v'_2 + \cdots\cdots$$

The product of these series is the convergent series

$$u'_0 v'_0 + u'_0 v'_1 + u'_1 v'_0 + u'_0 v'_2 + \cdots\cdots$$

But this series is precisely the series of absolute values of (α), and therefore (α) converges absolutely. It remains to show that the value toward which it converges is UV. Since S_N approaches a limit when N, increasing, passes through *all* integral values, S_N will continue to approach a limit, and this will be the same limit, if N passes only through the values n^2:

$$\lim_{N=\infty} S_N = \lim_{n=\infty} S_{n^2}.$$

But

$$S_{n^2} = s_n t_n \qquad \text{and} \qquad \lim_{n=\infty} S_{n^2} = UV.$$

This proves the theorem.

* The case that some of the terms are 0 must not however be excluded; hence the double sign ($\leqq$) in the inequality below: $S_N \leqq s_{n+1} t_{n+1}$.

For example, let

$$f(x) = a_0 + a_1x + a_2x^2 + \cdots\cdots,$$
$$\phi(x) = b_0 + b_1x + b_2x^2 + \cdots\cdots$$

be two convergent power series, x any point lying at once within the region of convergence of both series. Then the product of these series is given by the formula

$$f(x)\,\phi(x) = a_0b_0 + (a_0b_1 + a_1b_0)x + (a_0b_2 + a_1b_1 + a_2b_0)x^2 + \cdots\cdots$$

This formula can be used to give the square, or by repeated application, any power of a power series. Thus it gives as the square of the geometric series

$$1 + x + x^2 + \cdots\cdots$$

the series

$$1 + 2x + 3x^2 + \cdots\cdots,$$

a result agreeing with the binomial expansion of $(1 + x)^{-2}$.

Exercise. Find the first four terms in the expansion of

$$e^{-x}\sin x\cos x - \frac{x}{\sqrt{1 - x^2}} \qquad \text{and} \qquad \frac{\log(1 + x)}{1 + x}$$

Square the series for e^x and show that the result agrees with the expansion of e^{2x}.

36. One more theorem is extremely useful in practice. Its proof would carry us beyond the bounds of this chapter.

Let

$$\phi_n(y) = b_0 + b_1y + b_2y^2 + \cdots\cdots + b_ny^n$$

be any polynomial in y and let y be given by the convergent power series in x:

$$y = a_0 + a_1x + a_2x^2 + \cdots\cdots$$

Then the powers of y: y^2, y^3, $\cdots\cdots$ y^n can be obtained at once as power series in x by repeated multiplications of the x-series by itself, the terms of the polynomial $\phi_n(y)$ then formed by multiplying these power series respectively by the cofficients b, and the polynomial $\phi_n(y)$ thus represented as a power series in x by the addition of these terms.

Suppose however that instead of the polynomial $\phi_n(y)$ we had an infinite series:

$$\phi(y) = b_0 + b_1y + b_2y^2 + \cdots\cdots$$

Under what restrictions can the above process of representing $\phi_n(y)$ as a power series in x be extended to representing $\phi(y)$ as a power series in x?

One restriction is immediately obvious. Since a power series represents a continuous function (v. § 38) the values of y corresponding to small values of x will lie near to a_0 and *thus the point a_0 must surely lie within the interval of convergence* $(-r < y < r)$ *of the series* $\phi(y)$. Suppose $a_0 = 0$; then this condition is always satisfied. And now our theorem is precisely this, that no further condition is necessary.

THEOREM 4. *If $a_0 = 0$, no further restriction is necessary; i.e. the above process of representing $\phi(y)$ as a power series in x is always applicable.**

Remark. The point of the theorem just quoted is this. We know from § 35 that each term in the y series can be expressed as a power series in x:

$$b_n y^n = f_n(x) = a_0^{(n)} + a_1^{(n)} x + a_2^{(n)} x^2 + \cdots\cdots$$

and hence that $\phi(y)$ can be expressed in the form

$$\phi(y) = f_0(x) + f_1(x) + f_2(x) + \cdots\cdots$$

It remains to prove (and it is precisely this fact that the theorem asserts, — a fact not true in general of a convergent series of the form

$$f_0(x) + f_1(x) + f_2(x) + \cdots\cdots,$$

where $f_n(x)$ denotes a power series) that if we collect from these series all the terms of common degree in x and then rearrange them in the form of a single power series, first, this series will converge, and secondly, its value will be $\phi(y)$.

Examples. 1. Let it be required to develop $e^{x \sin x}$ according to powers of x.† Let $y = x \sin x$. Then

$$\phi(y) = e^y = 1 + y + \tfrac{1}{2} y^2 + \tfrac{1}{6} y^3 + \tfrac{1}{24} y^4 + \cdots\cdots$$

$$\begin{aligned}
y &= x^2 - \tfrac{1}{6} x^4 + \tfrac{1}{120} x^6 - \tfrac{1}{5040} x^8 + \cdots\cdots \\
\tfrac{1}{2} y^2 &= \qquad\quad \tfrac{1}{2} x^4 - \tfrac{1}{6} x^6 \quad + \tfrac{1}{45} x^8 + \cdots\cdots \\
\tfrac{1}{6} y^3 & \qquad\qquad\qquad\quad \tfrac{1}{6} x^6 \quad - \tfrac{1}{12} x^8 + \cdots\cdots \\
\tfrac{1}{24} y^4 & \qquad\qquad\qquad\qquad\qquad\quad \tfrac{1}{24} x^8 + \cdots\cdots \\
\cdot \quad & \cdot \quad \cdot \quad \cdot \quad \cdot \quad \cdot \quad \cdot \quad \cdot \quad \cdot \\
e^{x \sin x} &= 1 + x^2 + \tfrac{1}{3} x^4 + \tfrac{1}{120} x^6 - \tfrac{11}{560} x^8 + \cdots\cdots
\end{aligned}$$

* The case $a_0 = 0$ is the one that usually arises in practice. But the theorem still holds provided only that $-r < a_0 < r$, the only difference being that the coefficients in the final series will then be infinite series instead of sums. Cf. Stolz, *Allgemeine Arithmetik*, Vol. I, Ch. X, § 25.

† Even when it is known that a function can be developed by Taylor's Theorem (v. Ch. III; *Diff. Cal.*, Ch. IX; *Int. Cal.*, Ch. XVII) it is usually simpler to determine the coefficients in the series by the method here set forth than by performing the successive differentiations requisite in the application of Taylor's formula. The example in hand illustrates the truth of this statement.

2. Find the first 4 terms in the expansion of $\sin(k\sin x)$.

3. Obtain a few terms in the development of each of the following functions according to powers of x.

$$\log\cos x.$$

Suggestion. Let $\cos x = 1 + y$; then

$$y = -\tfrac{1}{2}x^2 + \tfrac{1}{24}x^4 - \cdots\cdots$$

and $$\log\cos x = -\tfrac{1}{2}x^2 - \tfrac{1}{12}x^4 - \tfrac{1}{45}x^6 + \cdots\cdots$$

$$\sqrt{\cos x}, \qquad \log(1 + e^x),$$

$$\frac{1}{\sqrt{1 - 2x\cos\theta + x^2}}, \qquad \frac{1}{\sqrt{1 - k^2\sin^2 x}}.$$

Theorem 4 gives no exact information concerning the extent of the region of convergence of the final series. It merely asserts that there is such a region. This deficiency is supplied by an elementary theorem in the Theory of Functions.*

But for many applications it is not necessary to know the exact region of convergence. For example, let it be required to determine the following limit.

$$\lim_{x=0} \frac{\log\cos x + 1 - \dfrac{1}{\sqrt{1 + x^2 + x^3}}}{\sin x - x}$$

Both numerator and denominator can be developed according to powers of x. The fraction then takes on the form

$$\frac{\tfrac{1}{2}x^3 + \text{higher powers of } x}{-\tfrac{1}{6}x^3 + \text{higher powers of } x}$$

Cancel x^3 from numerator and denominator and then let x approach 0 as its limit. The limit of the fraction is then seen to be -3. The usual method for dealing with the limit $0/0$ is applicable here, but the method of series gives a briefer solution, as the student can readily verify.

Example. Determine the limit

$$\lim_{x=0} \frac{\sqrt{a^2 - x^2} - \sqrt{a^2 + x^2}}{1 - \cos x}.$$

An important application of Theorem 4 is to the proof of the following theorem.

* Cf. *Int. Cal.*, § 220; *Higher Mathematics*, Ch. VI, Functions of a Complex Variable, by Thos. S. Fiske; John Wiley & Sons.

THEOREM. *The quotient of two power series can be represented as a power series, provided the constant term in the denominator series is not 0:*

$$\frac{b_0 + b_1 x + b_2 x^2 + \cdots\cdots}{a_0 + a_1 x + a_2 x^2 + \cdots\cdots} = c_0 + c_1 x + c_2 x^2 + \cdots\cdots,$$

$$\text{if } a_0 \neq 0.$$

It is sufficient to show that

$$\frac{1}{a_0 + a_1 x + a_2 x^2 + \cdots\cdots}$$

can be so represented, for then the power series that represents it can be multiplied into the numerator series

$$b_0 + b_1 x + b_2 x^2 + \cdots\cdots$$

Let

$$y = a_1 x + a_2 x^2 + \cdots\cdots$$

$$\frac{1}{a_0 + y} = \frac{1}{a_0} \cdot \frac{1}{1 + \frac{y}{a_0}} = \frac{1}{a_0} - \frac{y}{a_0^2} + \frac{y^2}{a_0^3} - \frac{y^3}{a_0^4} + \cdots\cdots,$$

provided y/a_0 is numerically less than unity, i. e. y numerically less than a_0. Thus the conditions of Theorem 4 are fulfilled and the function $1/(a_0 + y)$ can be expressed as a power series in x by developing each term $(-1)^n y^n/a_{n+1}$ into such a series and collecting from these series the terms of like degree in x.

COROLLARY. *If the coefficients of the first m powers of x in the denominator series vanish, the quotient can be expressed in the form*

$$\frac{b_0 + b_1 x + b_2 x^2 + \cdots\cdots}{a_m x^m + a_{m+1} x^{m+1} + \cdots\cdots} = \frac{C_{-m}}{x^m} + \frac{C_{-m+1}}{x^{m-1}} + \cdots\cdots + \frac{C_{-1}}{x} +$$

$$C_0 + C_1 x + C_2 x^2 + \cdots\cdots$$

For

$$\frac{b_0 + b_1 x + b_2 x^2 + \cdots\cdots}{a_m x^m + a_{m+1} x^{m+1} + \cdots\cdots} = \frac{1}{x^m} \cdot \frac{b_0 + b_1 x + b_2 x_2 + \cdots\cdots}{a_m + a_{m+1} x + \cdots\cdots\cdots}$$

$$= \frac{1}{x^m}(c_0 + c_1 x + c_2 x^2 + \cdots\cdots)$$

and it only remains to set $c_n = C_{n-m}$ and divide x^m into each term.

Examples. Show that

$$\tan x = x + \frac{1}{3} x^3 + \frac{2}{15} x^5 + \cdots\cdots,$$

$$\operatorname{ctn} x = \frac{1}{x} - \frac{1}{3} x - \frac{1}{45} x^3 + \cdots\cdots$$

and develop sec x and csc x to three terms.

A more convenient mode of determining the coefficients in these expansions will be given in § 37.

V. CONTINUITY, INTEGRATION AND DIFFERENTIATION OF SERIES.

37. *Continuity.* We have had numerous examples in the foregoing of continuous functions represented by power series. Is the converse true, namely, that every power series represents, within its interval of convergence, a continuous function? That this question is by no means trivial is shown by the fact that while the continuous functions of ordinary analysis can be represented (within certain limits) by trigonometric series, i. e. by series of the form

$$a_0 + a_1 \cos x + a_2 \cos 2x + \cdots\cdots$$
$$+ b_1 \sin x + b_2 \sin 2x + \cdots\cdots$$

a trigonometric series does *not* necessarily, conversely, represent a continuous function throughout its interval of convergence.

Let us first put into precise form what is meant by a *continuous function.* $\phi(x)$ is said to be continuous at the point x_0 if

$$\lim_{x = x_0} \phi(x) = \phi(x_0);$$

i. e. if, a belt being marked off bounded by the lines $y = \phi(x_0) + \epsilon$ and $y = \phi(x_0) - \epsilon$, where ϵ is an arbitrarily small positive quantity,

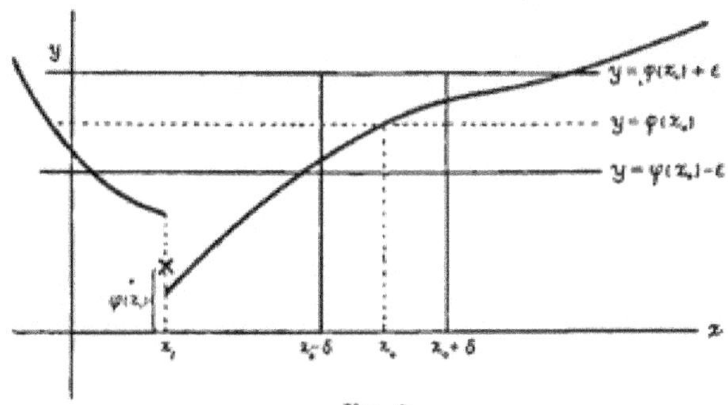

Fig. 8.

an interval $(x_0 - \delta, x_0 + \delta)$, $\delta > 0$, can then always be found such that, when x lies within this interval, $\phi(x)$ will lie within this belt. These conditions can be expressed in the following form:

$$\phi(x_0) - \epsilon < \phi(x) < \phi(x_0) + \epsilon, \qquad x_0 - \delta < x < x_0 + \delta;$$

or* $\qquad | \phi(x) - \phi(x_0) | < \epsilon, \qquad | x - x_0 | < \delta.$

A simple sufficient condition that the series of continuous functions

$$u_0(x) + u_1(x) + \cdots\cdots$$

represent a continuous function is given by the following theorem.

THEOREM 1. *If*

$$u_0(x) + u_1(x) + \cdots\cdots, \qquad \alpha \leqq x \leqq \beta,$$

is a series of continuous functions convergent throughout the interval (α, β), *then the function* $f(x)$ *represented by this series will be continuous throughout this interval, if a set of positive numbers,* M_0, M_1, M_2, $\cdots\cdots$, *independent of* x, *can be found such that*

1) $| u_n(x) | \leqq M_n, \quad \alpha \leqq x \leqq \beta, \quad n = 0, 1, 2, \cdots\cdots;$

2) $\qquad M_0 + M_1 + M_2 + \cdots\cdots$

is a convergent series.

We have to show that, x_0 being any point of the interval, if a positive quantity ϵ be chosen at pleasure, then a second positive quantity δ can be so determined that

$$| f(x) - f(x_0) | < \epsilon, \qquad \text{if} \qquad | x - x_0 | < \delta.$$

Let

$$s_n(x) = u_0(x) + u_1(x) + \cdots\cdots + u_{n-1}(x),$$

$$f(x) = s_n(x) + r_n(x).$$

Then

$$f(x) - f(x_0) = \{ s_n(x) - s_n(x_0) \} + r_n(x) - r_n(x_0).$$

We will show that the absolute value of each of the quantities $\{ s_n(x) - s_n(x_0) \}$, $r_n(x)$, $r_n(x_0)$ is less than $\frac{1}{3}\epsilon$, if δ is properly chosen and $| x - x_0 | < \delta$. From this follows that the absolute value of $f(x) - f(x_0)$ is less than ϵ; hence the proposition.

Let the remainder in the M-series be denoted by R_n:

$$R_n = M_n + M_{n+1} + \cdots\cdots;$$

and let n be so chosen that $R_n < \frac{1}{3}\epsilon$, and then held fast. Then, since

$$| u_n(x) | \leqq M_n,$$

$$| u_{n+1}(x) | \leqq M_{n+1},$$

$$\cdot \quad \cdot \quad \cdot \quad \cdot \quad \cdot \quad \cdot$$

it follows that

$$| r_n(x) | \leqq R_n$$

* The absolute value of a quantity A shall from now on be denoted by $| A |$.

*for all values of x at once,** or

$$|r_n(x)| < \tfrac{1}{3}\epsilon, \qquad \alpha \leqq x \leqq \beta.$$

Since $s_n(x)$ is the sum of a fixed number of continuous functions, it is a continuous function and hence δ can be so chosen that

$$|s_n(x) - s_n(x_0)| < \tfrac{1}{3}\epsilon, \qquad |x - x_0| < \delta.$$

Hence

$$|f(x) - f(x_0)| < \epsilon, \qquad |x - x_0| < \delta,$$

and the theorem is proved.

Exercise. Show that the series

$$\frac{\sin x}{1^2} - \frac{\sin 3x}{3^2} + \frac{\sin 5x}{5^2} - \cdots\cdots$$

converges and represents a continuous function.

38. The general test for continuity just obtained can be applied at once to power series

THEOREM 2. *A power series represents a continuous function within its interval of convergence. The function may however become discontinuous on the boundary of the interval.*

Let the series be

$$f(x) = a_0 + a_1 x + a_2 x^2 + \cdots\cdots,$$

convergent when $-r < x < r$; and let (α, β) be any interval contained in the interval of convergence, neither extremity coinciding with an extremity of that interval. Let X be chosen greater than either of the quantities $|\alpha|$, $|\beta|$, but less than r. Then

$$|a_n x^n| < |a_n| X^n, \qquad \alpha \leqq x \leqq \beta;$$

and the series

$$|a_0| + |a_1| X + |a_2| X^2 + \cdots\cdots$$

converges. Hence if we set

$$M_n = |a_n| X^n,$$

the conditions of Theorem 1 will be satisfied and therefore $f(x)$ is continuous throughout the interval (α, β).

By the aid of this theorem the following theorem can be readily proved.

* It is just at this point that the restriction on a convergent series of continuous functions, which the theorem imposes, comes into play. Without this restriction this proof would be impossible and in fact, as has already been pointed out, the theorem is not always true.

THEOREM. *If a power series vanishes for all values of x lying in a certain interval about the point $x = 0$:*

$$0 = a_0 + a_1 x + a_2 x^2 + \cdots\cdots, \qquad -l < x < l,$$

then each coefficient vanishes:

$$a_0 = 0, \quad a_1 = 0, \quad \cdots\cdots$$

First put $x = 0$; then $a_0 = 0$ and the above equation can be written in the form

$$0 = x(a_1 + a_2 x + \cdots\cdots)$$

From this equation it follows that

$$0 = a_1 + a_2 x + \cdots\cdots$$

provided $x \neq 0$; but it does not follow that this last equation is satisfied when $x = 0$, and therefore a_1 cannot be shown to vanish by putting $x = 0$ here as in the previous case. Theorem 2 furnishes a convenient means of meeting this difficulty. Let

$$f_1(x) = a_1 + a_2 x + \cdots\cdots$$

Then since $f_1(x)$ is by that theorem a continuous function of x

$$\lim_{x=0} f_1(x) = f_1(0) = a_1 .$$

But $\qquad \lim_{x=0} f_1(x) = 0; \qquad\qquad a_1 = 0 .$

By repeating this reasoning each of the subsequent coefficients can be shown to be 0, and thus the theorem is established.

COROLLARY. *If two power series have the same value for all values of x in an interval about the point $x = 0$, their coefficients are respectively equal:*

$$a_0 + a_1 x + a_2 x^2 + \cdots\cdots = b_0 + b_1 x + b_2 x^2 + \cdots\cdots; \quad -l < x < l,$$

$$a_0 = b_0, \qquad a_1 = b_1, \qquad \text{etc.}$$

Transpose one series to the other side of the equation and the proof is at once obvious.

The Determination of the Coefficients c. It was shown in § 36 that the quotient of two power series can be represented as a power series.

$$\frac{b_0 + b_1 x + b_2 x^2 + \cdots\cdots}{a_0 + a_1 x + a_2 x^2 + \cdots\cdots} = c_0 + c_1 x + c_2 x^2 + \cdots\cdots$$

By the aid of the theorems of this paragraph a more convenient mode of determining the coefficients c can be established. Multiply each side of the equation by the denominator series:

$$b_0+b_1x+b_2x^2+\cdots=(a_0+a_1x+a_2x^2+\cdots)(c_0+c_1x+c_2x^2+\cdots)$$
$$=a_0c_0+(a_1c_0+a_0c_1)x+(a_2c_0+a_1c_1+a_0c_2)x^2+\cdots\cdots$$

Hence
$$\begin{aligned} b_0 &= a_0c_0 \\ b_1 &= a_1c_0+a_0c_1 \\ b_2 &= a_2c_0+a_1c_1+a_0c_2 \\ &\cdot\quad\cdot\quad\cdot\quad\cdot\quad\cdot\quad\cdot \end{aligned}$$

A simple mode of solving these equations for the successive c's is furnished by the rule of elementary algebra for dividing one polynomial by another.

Quotient: $c_0+c_1x+c_2x^2+\cdots\cdots$

Divisor: $a_0+a_1x+a_2x^2+a_3x^3+\cdots\cdots$

$$\begin{array}{l}
b_0+b_1x+b_2x^2+b_3x^3+\cdots\cdots \\
a_0c_0 \quad a_1c_0 \quad a_2c_0 \quad a_3c_0 \\
\hline
(b_0-a_0c_0)+(b_1-a_1c_0)x+(b_2-a_2c_0)x^2+(b_3-a_3c_0)x^3+\cdots\cdots \\
\qquad a_0c_1 \qquad a_1c_1 \qquad a_2c_1 \\
\hline
(b_1-a_1c_0-a_0c_1)x+(b_2-a_2c_0-a_1c_1)x^2+(b_3-a_3c_0-a_2c_1)x^3+\cdots \\
\qquad a_0c_2 \qquad a_1c_2 \\
\hline
(b_2-a_2c_0-a_1c_1-a_0c_2)x^2+(b_3-a_3c_0-a_2c_1-a_1c_2)x^3+\cdots\cdots \\
\text{etc.}
\end{array}$$

The equations determining the c's are precisely the condition that the first term in the remainder shall vanish each time.

For example, to develop $\tan x$, divide the series for $\sin x$ by the series for $\cos x$.

Quotient: $x+\frac{1}{3}x^3+\frac{2}{15}x^5+\cdots\cdots$

Divisor: $1-\frac{1}{2}x^2+\frac{1}{24}x^4-\cdots\cdots$

$$\begin{array}{l}
x-\frac{1}{6}x^3+\frac{1}{120}x^5+\cdots\cdots \\
x-\frac{1}{2}x^3+\frac{1}{24}x^5+\cdots\cdots \\
\hline
\quad \frac{1}{3}x^3-\frac{1}{30}x^5+\cdots\cdots \\
\quad \frac{1}{3}x^3-\frac{1}{6}x^5+\cdots\cdots \\
\hline
\qquad \frac{2}{15}x^5+\cdots\cdots \\
\qquad \frac{2}{15}x^5+\cdots\cdots \\
\hline
\qquad \text{etc.}
\end{array}$$

Hence
$$\tan x = x+\tfrac{1}{3}x^3+\tfrac{2}{15}x^5+\cdots\cdots$$

This method is applicable even to the case treated in the corollary, § 36.

Exercise. Develop

$$\frac{1}{1+x}, \qquad \frac{12-5x+x^3}{3+x+x^7}, \qquad \csc^2 x.$$

39. *The Integration of Series Term by Term.* Let the continuous function $f(x)$ be represented by an infinite series of continuous functions convergent throughout the interval (α, β):

$$f(x) = u_0(x) + u_1(x) + \cdots\cdots, \qquad \alpha \leqq x \leqq \beta. \quad (A)$$

The problem is this: to determine when the integral of $f(x)$ will be given by the series of the integrals of the terms on the right of equation (A); i. e. to determine when

$$\int_\alpha^\beta f(x)\,dx = \int_\alpha^\beta u_0(x)\,dx + \int_\alpha^\beta u_1(x)\,dx + \cdots\cdots \quad (B)$$

will be a true equation. The right hand member of (B) is called the *term by term integral* of the u-series.

Let

$$s_n(x) = u_0(x) + u_1(x) + \cdots\cdots + u_{n-1}(x),$$

$$f(x) = s_n(x) + r_n(x).$$

Then

$$\int_\alpha^\beta f(x)\,dx = \int_\alpha^\beta s_n(x)\,dx + \int_\alpha^\beta r_n(x)\,dx$$

or

$$\int_\alpha^\beta f(x)\,dx = \int_\alpha^\beta u_0(x)\,dx + \int_\alpha^\beta u_1(x)\,dx + \cdots\cdots + \int_\alpha^\beta u_{n-1}(x)\,dx$$
$$+ \int_\alpha^\beta r_n(x)\,dx.$$

Hence *the necessary and sufficient condition that (B) is a true equation is that*

$$\lim_{n=\infty} \int_\alpha^\beta r_n(x)\,dx = 0.$$

To obtain a test for determining when this condition is satisfied, plot the curve

$$y = r_n(x).$$

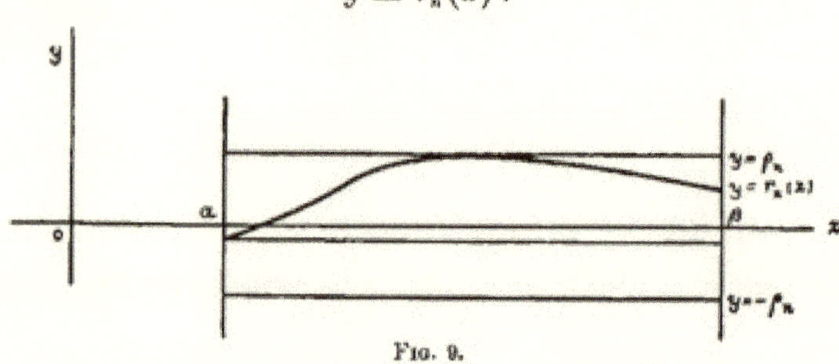

Fig. 9.

The area under this curve will represent geometrically

$$\int_\alpha^\beta r_n(x)\,dx.$$

Draw lines through the highest and lowest points of the curve parallel to the x-axis. The distance ρ_n of the more remote of these lines from the x-axis is the maximum value that $|r_n(x)|$ attains in the interval. Lay off a belt bounded by the lines $y = \rho_n$ and $y = -\rho_n$. Then the curve lies wholly within this belt and the absolute value of the area under the curve cannot exceed the area of the rectangle bounded by the line $y = \rho_n$, or $(\beta - \alpha)\rho_n$. This area will converge toward 0 as its limit if *

$$\lim_{n=\infty} \rho_n = 0,$$

and thus we shall have a *sufficient* condition for the truth of equation (B) if we establish a sufficient condition that the maximum value ρ_n of $|r_n(x)|$ in the interval (α, β) approaches 0 when $n = \infty$. Now we saw in the proof of Theorem 1 that if the series (A) satisfies the conditions of that theorem,

$$|r_n(x)| \leqq R_n, \qquad \alpha \leqq x \leqq \beta, \qquad \lim_{n=\infty} R_n = 0.$$

Hence any such series can be integrated term by term and we have in this result a test sufficiently general for most of the cases that arise in ordinary practice. Let the test be formulated as follows.

THEOREM 3. *Series (A) can always be integrated term by term, i. e.*

$$\int_\alpha^\beta f(x)\,dx = \int_\alpha^\beta u_0(x)\,dx + \int_\alpha^\beta u_1(x)\,dx + \cdots\cdots$$

will be a true equation, if a set of positive numbers $M_0, M_1, M_2, \ldots\ldots$, independent of x, can be found such that

1) $|u_n(x)| \leqq M_n, \qquad \alpha \leqq x \leqq \beta, \qquad n = 0, 1, 2, \cdots\cdots;$

2) $$M_0 + M_1 + M_2 + \cdots\cdots$$

is a convergent series.

The form in which the test has been deduced is restricted to real functions of a real variable. But the theorem itself is equally applicable to complex variables and functions. It is desirable therefore to give a proof that applies at once to both cases.

* This condition is not satisfied by all series that are subject merely to the restrictions hitherto imposed on (A). Not every series of this sort can be integrated term by term. See an article by the author: *A Geometrical Method for the Treatment of Uniform Convergence and Certain Double Limits*, Bulletin of the Amer. Math. Soc., 2d ser., vol. iii, Nov. 1896, where examples of series that cannot be integrated term by term are given and the nature of such series is discussed by the aid of graphical methods.

Keeping the notation used above, the relation

$$\int_\alpha^\beta f(x)\,dx = \int_\alpha^\beta u_0(x)\,dx + \int_\alpha^\beta u_1(x)\,dx + \cdots\cdots + \int_\alpha^\beta u_{n-1}(x)\,dx + \int_\alpha^\beta r_n(x)\,dx$$

still holds and the proof of the theorem turns on showing that the hypotheses are sufficient to enable us to infer that

$$\lim_{n=\infty} \int_\alpha^\beta r_n(x)\,dx = 0\,.$$

Let the remainder of the M-series be denoted as in § 37 by R_n:

$$R_n = M_n + M_{n+1} + \cdots\cdots$$

Then it follows, as in that paragraph, that

$$|\, r_n(x) \,| \leqq R_n\,.$$

Now

$$\left| \int_\alpha^\beta r_n(x)\,dx \right| \leqq \int_\alpha^\beta |\, r_n(x) \,| \cdot |\, dx \,| < R_n l\,,$$

the second integral being extended along the same path as the first, and l denoting the length of the path. But $\lim\limits_{n=\infty} (R_n l) = 0$; hence $\int_\alpha^\beta r_n(x)\,dx$ converges toward 0 when $n = \infty$ and the proof is complete.

40. We proceed now to apply the above test to the integration of some of the more common forms of series.

First Application: Power Series. A power series can be integrated term by term throughout any interval (α, β) *contained in the interval of convergence and not reaching out to the extremities of this interval:*

$$|\,\alpha\,| < r, \qquad |\,\beta\,| < r.$$

Let the series be written in the form

$$f(x) = a_0 + a_1 x + a_2 x^2 + \cdots\cdots$$

and let X be chosen greater than the greater of the two quantities $|\,\alpha\,|$, $|\,\beta\,|$, but less than r. Then

$$|\, a_n x^n \,| < |\, a_n \,|\, X^n, \qquad \alpha \leqq x \leqq \beta,$$

and if we set

$$|\, a_n \,|\, X^n = M_n\,,$$

the conditions of the test will be satisfied.

In particular

$$\int_0^h f(x)\,dx = a_0 h + a_1\frac{h^2}{2} + a_2\frac{h^3}{3} + \cdots\cdots, \qquad |h| < r.$$

If when $x = r$ or $-r$, the series for $f(x)$ converges absolutely, then h may be taken equal to r or $-r$. If however the series for $f(x)$ does not converge absolutely or diverges when $x = r$ or $-r$, it may nevertheless happen that the integral series converges when $h = r$ or $-r$. In this case the value of the integral series will still be the integral of $f(x)$. Thus the series

$$\frac{1}{1+x} = 1 - x + x^2 - x^3 + \cdots\cdots$$

diverges when $x = 1$; but the equation

$$\int_0^h \frac{dx}{1+x} = h - \frac{h^2}{2} + \frac{h^3}{3} - \cdots\cdots$$

still holds when $h = 1$:

$$\log 2 = 1 - \tfrac{1}{2} + \tfrac{1}{3} - \tfrac{1}{4} + \cdots\cdots$$

The proof of this theorem will be omitted.

Second Application: Series of Powers of a Function. Let $\phi(x)$ be a continuous function of x and let its maximum and minimum values lie between $-r$ and r when $a \leqq x \leqq \beta$. Let the power series

$$a_0 + a_1 y + a_2 y^2 + \cdots\cdots$$

converge when $-r < y < r$. Then the series

$$f(x) = a_0 + a_1\phi(x) + a_2[\phi(x)]^2 + \cdots\cdots$$

can be integrated term by term from a to β:

$$\int_a^\beta f(x)\,dx = a_0\int_a^\beta dx + a_1\int_a^\beta \phi(x)\,dx + a_2\int_a^\beta [\phi(x)]^2 dx + \cdots\cdot$$

For if Y be so taken that it is greater than the numerically greatest value of $\phi(x)$ in the interval $a \leqq x \leqq \beta$, but less than r, then

1) $$|a_n|\;|\phi(x)|^n < |a_n|\,Y^n,$$

2) $$|a_0| + |a_1|\,Y + |a_2|\,Y^2 + \cdots\cdots$$

converges; and if we set

$$|a_n|\,Y^n = M_n,$$

the conditions of the test will be satisfied.

Thus the integrations of §§ 24, 25 are justified.

Third Application. If the function $\phi(x)$ *and the series*

$$a_0 + a_1 y + a_2 y^2 + \cdots\cdots$$

satisfy the same conditions as in the preceding theorem and if $\psi(x)$ *is any continuous function of* x, *then the series*

$$f(x) = a_0\psi(x) + a_1\psi(x)\,\phi(x) + a_2\psi(x)\,[\phi(x)]^2 + \cdots\cdots$$

can be integrated term by term.

The method of proof has been so fully illustrated in the two preceding applications that the detailed construction of the proof may be left as an exercise to the student.

This theorem is needed in the deduction of Taylor's Theorem from Cauchy's Integral.

Examples. 1. Compute

$$\int_0^1 x^{\frac{1}{2}} e^{-x}\,dx, \qquad \int_0^{\frac{\pi}{2}} \sqrt{\sin x}\,dx.$$

2. Show that

$$\frac{1}{\pi}\int_0^\pi \cos(x\sin\phi)\,d\phi = 1 - \frac{x^2}{2^2} + \frac{x^4}{2^4(2\,!)^2} - \frac{x^6}{2^6(3\,!)^2} + \cdots\cdots$$

Hitherto the limits of integration have always been the limits of the interval considered, α and β. It becomes evident on a little reflection that if any other limits of integration, x_0, x, lying within the interval (α, β) are taken, Theorem 3 will still hold:

$$\int_{x_0}^{x} f(x)\,dx = \int_{x_0}^{x} u_0(x)\,dx + \int_{x_0}^{x} u_1(x)\,dx + \cdots\cdots$$

$$\alpha \leqq x_0 \leqq \beta, \qquad \alpha \leqq x \leqq \beta.$$

For, all the conditions of the test will hold for the interval (x_0, x) if they hold for the interval (α, β).

41. *The Differentiation of Series Term by Term. Let the function* $f(x)$ *be represented by the series:*

$$f(x) = u_0(x) + u_1(x) + \cdots\cdots$$

throughout the interval (α, β). *Then the derivative* $f'(x)$ *will be given at any point of the interval by the series of the derivatives:*

$$f'(x) = u'_0(x) + u'_1(x) + \cdots\cdots$$

provided the series of the derivatives

$$u'_0(x) + u'_1(x) + \cdots\cdots$$

satisfies the conditions of Theorem 1 throughout the interval (α, β).

Let the latter series be denoted by $\phi(x)$:

$$\phi(x) = u'_0(x) + u'_1(x) + \cdot \cdot \cdot \cdot \cdot$$

We wish to prove that

$$\phi(x) = f'(x).$$

By Theorem 1 the function $\phi(x)$ represented by the u'-series is continuous and by Theorem 2 the series can be integrated term by term:

$$\int_a^x \phi(x)\,dx = \int_a^x u'_0(x)\,dx + \int_a^x u'_1(x)\,dx + \cdot \cdot \cdot \cdot \cdot$$

$$= \{u_0(x) - u_0(a)\} + \{u_1(x) - u_1(a)\} + \cdot \cdot \cdot \cdot \cdot$$

$$= f(x) - f(a).$$

Hence, differentiating,

$$\phi(x) = f'(x), \qquad q.\ e.\ d.$$

Exercise. Show that the series

$$\frac{\cos x}{1^3} - \frac{\cos 3x}{1^3} + \frac{\cos 5x}{5^3} - \cdot \cdot \cdot \cdot \cdot$$

can be differentiated term by term.

By the aid of this general theorem we can at once prove the following theorem.

THEOREM. *A power series can be differentiated term by term at any point within (but not necessarily at a point on the boundary of) its interval of convergence.*

Let the power series be

$$f(x) = a_0 + a_1 x + a_2 x^2 + a_3 x^3 + \cdot \cdot \cdot \cdot \cdot,$$

convergent when $|x| < r$, and form the series of the derivatives:

$$a_1 + 2a_2 x + 3a_3 x^2 + \cdot \cdot \cdot \cdot \cdot$$

Then we want to prove that if $|x_0| < r$,

$$f'(x_0) = a_1 + 2a_2 x_0 + 3a_3 x_0^2 + \cdot \cdot \cdot \cdot \cdot$$

It will be sufficient to show that the series of the derivatives converges when $|x| < r$; for in that case, if X be so chosen that $|x_0| < X < r$, the conditions of the test will be fulfilled throughout the interval $(-X, X)$. We can prove this as follows. Let x' be any value of x within the interval $(-r, r)$: $-r < x' < r$, and let X' be so chosen that $|x'| < X' < r$. The series

$$|a_0| + |a_1| X' + |a_2| X'^2 + \cdot \cdot \cdot \cdot \cdot$$

converges. It will serve as a test-series for the convergence of

$$|a_1| + 2|a_2|\ |x'| + 3|a_3|\ |x'|^2$$

if it can be shown that

$$n\,|\,a_n\,|\;|\,x'\,|^{n-1} < |\,a_n\,|\,X'^n$$

from some definite point, $n = m$, on. This will be the case if

$$n\left(\frac{|\,x'\,|}{X'}\right)^n < |\,x'\,|, \qquad n > m.$$

But the expression on the left approaches 0 when $n = \infty$, for $|\,x'\,|\,/\,X'$ is independent of n and less than 1; the limit can therefore be obtained by the usual method for evaluating the limit $\infty \cdot 0$. Hence the condition that the former series may serve as test-series is fulfilled and the proof is complete.

Exercise. From the formula

$$\frac{1}{1-x} = 1 + x + x^2 + x^3 + \cdot \cdot \cdot \cdot \cdot$$

obtain by differentiation the developments for

$$\frac{1}{(1-x)^2}, \quad \frac{1}{(1-x)^3}, \quad \cdot \quad \cdot \quad \cdot \quad \frac{1}{(1-x)^n},$$

and show that they agree with the corresponding developments given by the binomial theorem.

APPENDIX.

A FUNDAMENTAL THEOREM REGARDING THE EXISTENCE OF A LIMIT.

It was shown in § 13 that if the variable s_n approaches a limit when n increases indefinitely, then

$$s_{n+p} - s_n$$

approaches the limit 0 when p is constant or varies in any wise with n. And it was stated that if, conversely, the limit of this expression is 0 when $n = \infty$, *no matter how we allow p to vary with n*, then s_n will approach a limit. This latter theorem is important in the theory of infinite series. It is however only a special case of a theorem regarding the existence of a limit, which is of fundamental importance in higher analysis.

THEOREM. *Let $f(x)$ be any function of x such that*

$$\lim\, [f(x') - f(x'')] = 0$$

when x' and x'', regarded as independent variables, both become infinite. Then $f(x)$ approaches a limit when $x = \infty$.

We will begin by stating precisely what we mean by saying that $f(x') - f(x'')$ approaches the limit 0 when x' and x'', regarded as independent variables, both become infinite. We mean that if X is taken as an independent variable that is allowed to increase without limit and then, corresponding to any given value of X, the pair of values (x', x'') is chosen arbitrarily subject only to the condition that both x' and x'' are greater than X (or at least as great), the quantity $f(x') - f(x'')$ will then converge towards 0 as its limit. In other words, let ϵ denote an arbitrarily small positive quantity. Then X can be so chosen that *

$$| f(x') - f(x'') | < \epsilon, \qquad \text{if} \qquad x' \geqq X \qquad \text{and } x'' \geqq X.$$

We proceed now to the proof. Let us choose for the successive values that ϵ is to take on any set $\epsilon_1, \epsilon_2, \epsilon_3, \ldots\ldots$ steadily decreasing and approaching the limit 0; — for example the values $1, \frac{1}{2}, \frac{1}{3}, \ldots\ldots, \epsilon_i = 1/i$. Denote the corresponding values of X by $X_1, X_2, X_3 \ldots\ldots$ Then in general these latter values will

* For the notation cf. foot-note, p. 53.

steadily increase, and we can in any case choose them so that they do always increase.

Begin by putting $\epsilon = \epsilon_1$:

$$|f(x') - f(x'')| < \epsilon_1, \qquad x' \geqq X_1, \qquad x'' \geqq X_1.$$

Assign to x' the value X_1. Then

$$|f(X_1) - f(x)| < \epsilon_1,$$

i. e.
$$f(X_1) - \epsilon_1 < f(x) < f(X_1) + \epsilon_1$$

for all values of x greater than X_1. The meaning of this last relation can be illustrated graphically as follows. Plot the point $f(X_1)$ on a line and mark the points $f(X_1) - \epsilon_1$ and $f(X_1) + \epsilon_1$. Then the inequalities assert that the point which represents $f(x)$ always lies within this interval, whose length is $2\epsilon_1$, provided $x > X_1$.

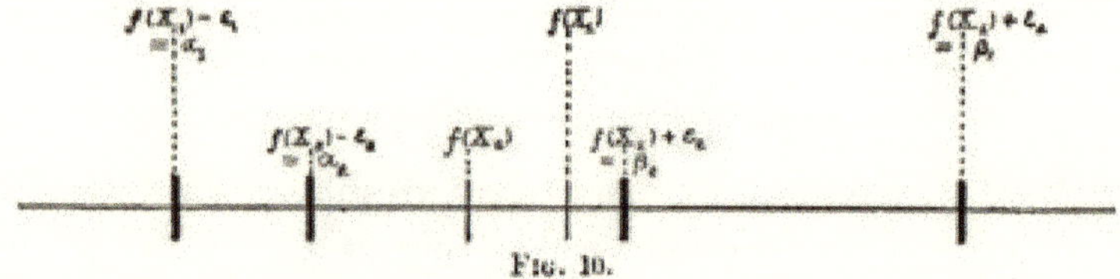

FIG. 10.

Denote the left hand boundary $f(X_1) - \epsilon_1$ of this interval by α_1, the right hand boundary $f(X_1) + \epsilon_1$ by β_1. Then, to restate concisely the foregoing results,

$$\alpha_1 < f(x) < \beta_1 \quad \text{if} \quad x > X_1; \qquad \beta_1 - \alpha_1 = 2\epsilon_1.$$

Now repeat this step, choosing for ϵ the value ϵ_2:

$$|f(X_2) - f(x)| < \epsilon_2,$$

i. e.
$$f(X_2) - \epsilon_2 < f(x) < f(X_2) + \epsilon_2,$$

where x denotes any value of the variable x greater than X_2. Plot the point $f(X_2)$; this point lies in the interval (α_1, β_1). Mark the points $f(X_2) - \epsilon_2$ and $f(X_2) + \epsilon_2$. Then three cases can arise:

(*a*) both of these points lie in the interval (α_1, β_1); let them be denoted respectively by α_2, β_2;

(*b*) $f(X_2)$ lies so near to α_1 that $f(X_2) - \epsilon_2$ falls outside the interval; in this case, let α_2 be taken coincident with α_1: $\alpha_2 = \alpha_1$; the other point $f(X_2) + \epsilon_2$ will lie in the interval (α_1, β_1) and shall be denoted by β_2;

(*c*) $f(X_2)$ lies so near to β_1 that $f(X_2) + \epsilon_2$ falls outside the interval; in this case, let β_2 be taken coincident with β_1: $\beta_2 = \beta_1$; the other point $f(X_2) - \epsilon_2$ will lie in the interval (α_1, β_1) and shall be denoted by α_2.

In each one of these three cases

$$\alpha_2 < f(x) < \beta_2 \quad \text{if} \quad x > X_2; \quad \beta_2 - \alpha_2 \leqq 2\epsilon_2.$$

The remainder of the proof is extremely simple. The step just described at length can be repeated again and again, and we shall have as the result in the general case the following:

$$\alpha_i < f(x) < \beta_i \quad \text{if} \quad x > X_i; \quad \beta_i - \alpha_i \leqq 2\epsilon_i.$$

Now consider the set of points that represent $\alpha_1, \alpha_2, \ldots \alpha_i, \ldots$ They advance in general toward the right as i increases, — they never recede toward the left, — but no one of them ever advances so far to the right as β_1. Hence, by the principle* of § 4, they opproach a limit A. Similar reasoning shows that the points representing $\beta_1, \beta_2, \ldots \beta_i, \ldots$ approach a limit B. And since

$$0 < \beta_i - \alpha_i \leqq 2\epsilon_i,$$

these limits must be equal: $A = B$.

From this it follows that $f(x)$ converges toward the same limit. For

$$\alpha_i < f(x) < \beta_i, \qquad x > X_i;$$

and if when x increases indefinitely, we allow i to increase indefinitely at the same time, but not so rapidly as to invalidate these inequalities, we see that $f(x)$ is shut in between two variables, α_i and β_i, each of which approaches the same limit. Hence $f(x)$ approaches that limit also, and the theorem is proved.

In the theorem in infinite series above quoted n is the independent variable x, s_n the function $f(x)$; the expression $s_{n+p} - s_n$ corresponds to $f(x') - f(x'')$; and thus that theorem is seen to be a special case of the theorem just proved. The domain of values for the variable x is in this case the positive integers, 1, 2, 3, ...

Another application of the present theorem is to the convergence of a definite integral when the upper limit becomes infinite. Let

$$f(x) = \int_a^x \phi(x)\,dx.$$

Then $$f(x') - f(x'') = \int_a^{x'} \phi(x)\,dx - \int_a^{x''} \phi(x)\,dx = \int_{x''}^{x'} \phi(x)\,dx.$$

Hence if $$\lim \int_{x''}^{x'} \phi(x)\,dx = 0$$

* This principle was stated, to be sure, in the form $S_{n'} > S$ if $n' > n$; but it obviously continues to hold if we assume merely that $S_{n'} \geqq S_n$ when $n' > n$.

when x' and x'', regarded as independent variables, both become infinite, the integral

$$\int_a^\infty \phi(x)\,dx$$

is convergent. The domain of values for the variable x is in this case all the real quantities greater than a.

In the foregoing theorem it has been assumed that the independent variable x increases without limit. The theorem can however be readily extended to the case that x decreases algebraically indefinitely or approaches a limit a from either side or from both sides. In the first case, let

$$x = -y;$$

in the second, let

$$x = a + \frac{1}{y}$$

if x is always greater than its limit a; let

$$x = a - \frac{1}{y}$$

if x is always less than a. Then if we set

$$f(x) = \phi(y)$$

and the function $\phi(y)$ satisfies the conditions of the theorem when $y = +\infty$, $\phi(y)$ and hence $f(x)$ will approach a limit. Finally, if x in approaching a assumes values sometimes greater than a and sometimes less, we may restrict x first to approaching a from above, secondly from below. In each of these cases it has just been seen that $f(x)$ approaches a limit, and since

$$\lim\,[f(x') - f(x'')] = 0$$

where x' and x'' may now be taken the one above, the other below a, these two limits must be equal. We are thus led to the following more general form of statement of the theorem.

THEOREM. *Let $f(x)$ be such a function of x that,*

$$\lim\,[f(x') - f(x'')] = 0$$

when x' and x'', regarded as independent variables, approach the limit a from above or from below or from both sides, or become positively or negatively infinite. Then $f(x)$ approaches a limit when x approaches the limit a from above or from below or from both sides, or becomes positively or negatively infinite.

A TABLE OF THE MORE IMPORTANT FORMULAS.

The heavy line indicates the region of convergence.

$$\frac{1}{1-x} = 1 + x + x^2 + x^3 + \cdots\cdots$$

−1 0 1

$$\frac{1}{a-bx} = \frac{1}{a} + \frac{b}{a^2}x + \frac{b^2}{a^3}x^2 + \frac{b^3}{a^4}x^3 + \cdots\cdots$$

−r 0 r

$r = \frac{a}{b}$ numerically.

$$\log(1+x) = x - \frac{x^2}{2} + \frac{x^3}{3} - \frac{x^4}{4} + \cdots\cdots$$

−1 0 1

$$\log\frac{1+x}{1-x} = 2\left(x + \frac{x^3}{3} + \frac{x^5}{5} + \cdots\cdots\right)$$

−1 0 1

$$(1+x)^\mu = 1 + \mu x + \frac{\mu(\mu-1)}{1\cdot 2}x^2 + \frac{\mu(\mu-1)(\mu-2)}{1\cdot 2\cdot 3}x^3 + \cdots\cdots$$

−1 0 1

$$\frac{1}{(1+x)^2} = 1 - 2x + 3x^2 - 4x^3 + \cdots\cdots$$

−1 0 1

$$\frac{1}{\sqrt{1-x^2}} = 1 + \frac{1}{2}x^2 + \frac{1\cdot 3}{2\cdot 4}x^4 + \frac{1\cdot 3\cdot 5}{2\cdot 4\cdot 6}x^6 + \cdots\cdots$$

−1 0 1

$$\sqrt{1-x^2} = 1 - \frac{1}{2}x^2 - \frac{1}{2\cdot 4}x^4 - \frac{1\cdot 3}{2\cdot 4\cdot 6}x^6 - \cdots\cdots$$

−1 0 1

$$e^x = 1 + x + \frac{x^2}{2\,!} + \frac{x^3}{3\,!} + \frac{x^4}{4\,!} + \cdots\cdots$$

−∞ 0 ∞

$$\sin x = x - \frac{x^3}{3\,!} + \frac{x^5}{5\,!} - \frac{x^7}{7\,!} + \cdots\cdots$$

−∞ 0 ∞

$$\cos x = 1 - \frac{x^2}{2\,!} + \frac{x^4}{4\,!} - \frac{x^6}{6\,!} + \cdots\cdots$$

−∞ 0 ∞

$$\tan x = x + \tfrac{1}{3}x^3 + \tfrac{2}{15}x^5 + \cdots\cdots$$

$-\frac{\pi}{2}$ 0 $\frac{\pi}{2}$

$$\cot x = \frac{1}{x} - \tfrac{1}{3}x - \tfrac{1}{45}x^3 + \cdots\cdots$$

$-\pi$ 0 π

$$\sec x = 1 + \tfrac{1}{2}x^2 + \tfrac{5}{24}x^4 + \cdots\cdots$$

$-\frac{\pi}{2}$ 0 $\frac{\pi}{2}$

$$\sin^{-1}x = x + \frac{1}{2}\frac{x^3}{3} + \frac{1\cdot 3}{2\cdot 4}\frac{x^5}{5} + \frac{1\cdot 3\cdot 5}{2\cdot 4\cdot 6}\frac{x^7}{7} + \cdots\cdots$$

-1 0 1

$$\tan^{-1}x = x - \frac{x^3}{3} + \frac{x^5}{5} - \frac{x^7}{7} + \cdots\cdots$$

-1 0 1

$$f(x_0+h) = f(x_0) + f'(x_0)\,h + f''(x_0)\frac{h^2}{2\,!} + \cdots\cdots + f^{(n)}(x_0+\theta h)\frac{h^n}{n\,!}$$

$$0 < \theta < 1$$

$$f(x_0+h) = f(x_0) + hf'(x_0+\theta h)$$

$$K = \int_0^{\frac{\pi}{2}} \frac{d\phi}{\sqrt{1-k^2\sin^2\phi}} =$$

$$\frac{\pi}{2}\left[1 + \left(\frac{1}{2}\right)^2 k^2 + \left(\frac{1\cdot 3}{2\cdot 4}\right)^2 k^4 + \left(\frac{1\cdot 3\cdot 5}{2\cdot 4\cdot 6}\right)^2 k^6 + \cdots\cdots\right]$$

$$E = \int_0^{\frac{\pi}{2}} \sqrt{1-k^2\sin^2\phi}\;d\phi =$$

$$\frac{\pi}{2}\left[1 - \left(\frac{1}{2}\right)^2 k^2 - \left(\frac{1\cdot 3}{2\cdot 4}\right)^2 \frac{k^4}{3} - \left(\frac{1\cdot 3\cdot 5}{2\cdot 4\cdot 6}\right)^2 \frac{k^6}{5} + \cdots\cdots\right]$$

For small values of x the following equations are approximately correct.

$$f(a+x) = f(a) + f'(a)\,x$$

$$(1+x)^m = 1 + mx$$

$$(1+x)^2 = 1 + 2x$$

$$\sqrt{1+x} = 1 + \tfrac{1}{2}x$$

$$\frac{1}{1+x} = 1 - x$$

$$\frac{1}{(1+x)^2} = 1 - 2x$$

$$\frac{1}{\sqrt{1+x}} = 1 - \tfrac{1}{2}x$$

If $x, y, z, w, \cdots\cdots$ are all numerically small, then, approximately,

$$(1+x)(1+y)(1+z)\cdots\cdots = 1 + x + y + z + \cdots\cdots$$

$$\frac{(1+x)(1+y)\cdots\cdots}{(1+z)(1+w)\cdots\cdots} = 1 + x + y\cdots\cdots - z - w - \cdots\cdots$$

$$\sin x = x \quad \text{or} \quad x - \tfrac{1}{6}x^3$$

$$\cos x = 1 \quad \text{or} \quad 1 - \tfrac{1}{2}x^2$$

$$\tan x = x \quad \text{or} \quad x + \tfrac{1}{3}x^3$$

$$\sin(a+x) - \sin a = x\cos a$$

$$\cos(a+x) - \cos a = -x\sin a$$

$$\log(a+x) - \log a = \frac{x}{a}$$

www.ingramcontent.com/pod-product-compliance
Lightning Source LLC
Chambersburg PA
CBHW020240090426
42735CB00010B/1771

* 9 7 8 3 7 4 3 3 0 5 1 4 4 *